BUILDING THE FACULTY WE NEED

Colleges and Universities Working Together

Jerry G. Gaff
Anne S. Pruitt-Logan
Richard A. Weibl
and participants in the
Preparing Future Faculty Program

The Preparing Future Faculty programs are sponsored by the Council of Graduate Schools and the Association of American Colleges and Universities. The programs are made possible with funding from the participating institutions and by grants from The Pew Charitable Trusts and the National Science Foundation.

Contents

Foreword

Soon after I accepted my new position as director of education for The Pew Charitable Trusts, my Pew colleague Ellen Wert called me to say that we had a decision to make. The Preparing Future Faculty (PFF) program launched in 1993 by Ellen and my predecessor, Bob Schwartz, was coming to the end of its initial support. Would I be supportive of another three-year grant? If so, it would be the biggest item on the education agenda of my first meeting with the Trusts' board.

The Association of American Colleges and Universities (AAC&U) hosted a meeting for all those involved on the project. Jules LaPidus and Anne Pruitt-Logan from the Council of Graduate Schools (CGS), and Carol Geary Schneider and Jerry Gaff from AAC&U faced Ellen and me as tough-minded foundation program officers, and we grilled them for two hours, from every angle we could think of.

I learned that PFF is built on the idea that readiness to enter the academic profession entails far more than disciplinary expertise.

I learned that, like most powerful ideas, PFF had grown out of streams of earlier work—the efforts of many campuses to improve the teaching capacity of TAs, the pioneering leadership of Syracuse University in conceiving TA training as a developmental process that can end with a certificate in university teaching, and the leadership of AAC&U in piloting the notion that those graduate students might benefit from a stint of mentored teaching in liberal arts colleges.

Furthermore, I learned that CGS and AAC&U had joined together to form a strong partnership that was extraordinary among educational associations in Washington D.C. With support from The Pew Charitable Trusts, they launched PFF. At the beginning, everyone was nervous that they might be throwing a party to which no one would come. What happened, instead, was that 70 of the 102 universities that produce significant numbers of Ph.D.s applied to the program. PFF had tapped into an energy source for graduate education reform that had been pent up for a long time. And I learned that in three short years, not only had the seventeen institutions initially selected done pioneering work, but many other institutions, without benefit of external support for doing so, had picked up the ideas of PFF and were running with them on their own.

It was, in the end, an easy call. With the intellectual leadership of the project directors, the endeavor would succeed. The commitment to continue was there. It is one thing, I argued, to stimulate institutions to develop their own variations on an organizing idea; it is quite another to then place these variations on a map and make sense of them.

In this manuscript is proof that, with the generous support of many others, of course, these are people who deliver. The writing is clear, clean, and straightforward. The perspective is that of a helicopter pilot flying over the terrain— high enough to see the forest, but also low enough to see the trees and the rough spots. It is not quite like watching an IMAX movie, but in reading this manuscript I had the feeling of joining the PFF expedition and being there. It is everything the Trusts had any right to hope for—and more.

From the perspective of this happy funder, PFF has been and continues to be a great success. As I write this foreword, fifteen institutions are scaling up PFF projects to the point that formal training experiences will be available to all of their graduate students who want them. PFF ideas have also spread into the disciplinary associations. The National Science Foundation is now funding a PFF program in mathematics and science, and, led by the National Communication Association, PFF projects are springing up in social science and humanities disciplines as well.

This is not to say that the journey is over, or that the final destination is even in sight. The Rockies are still ahead. PFF has added services and stirred new questions about what preparation for the twenty-first century professoriate should be. The next big challenge, it seems to me, is to rethink the nature of the Ph.D. itself so that PFF-type experiences are not add-ons but an integral part of every faculty member's doctoral portfolio. But enough of this. Today is for reading this report, looking back, and realizing with growing exhilaration how far this expedition has already come.

RUSSELL EDGERTON
Director, Education Program
The Pew Charitable Trusts

Preface

Expectations for college professors are rising, and the nature of academic work is changing. In their research, faculty members often must draw from findings and methods of other disciplines, and they are increasingly encouraged to use their specialized knowledge to address problems and needs in their communities. In teaching, they must work with a student body that is very diverse in their academic skills and motivations as well as their ethnic and racial cultures, and they are expected to utilize the powerful new technological, collaborative, and experiential approaches to teaching and learning. As professionals who are intimately involved in establishing policies for their organizations, they are expected to play a role in governing their own departments, institutions and professional associations.

Yet, doctoral education, which is where preparation for faculty work is primarily acquired, has not changed significantly to take account of these new realities. For too many graduate students, preparation for a faculty career still means essentially learning the content of a discipline, developing expertise in a specialization, and conducting a research project presented in a dissertation. For too many individuals, developing the capacity for teaching and learning about fundamental professional concepts and principles remain accidental occurrences. We can — and should — do a better job of building the faculty the nation's colleges and universities need.

This report offers a new vision of doctoral education for the professoriate. This vision is broader than the traditional preparation of students planning to become faculty members. It includes preparation for teaching and professional service as well as for research and opportunities to experience faculty life in a variety of colleges and universities. The report illustrates the way we, participants and leaders, have found that innovative faculty preparation programs work, the benefits they offer, and the implications they hold for the academy.

The Preparing Future Faculty (PFF) program serves as the foundation of this new vision. A joint undertaking of the Association of American Colleges and Universities and the Council of Graduate Schools, PFF has been supported since 1993 by The Pew Charitable Trusts. It was designed, first, to develop alternative models of faculty preparation (during Phase I, 1993–1997) and, then, to institutionalize them (Phase II, 1997–2000). With support from the National Science Foundation, PFF III was launched to develop model PFF programs in science and mathematics departments. PFF IV involves humanities and social sciences departments.

PFF grows out of dissatisfaction with traditional forms of faculty preparation, based on several beliefs about the ways college professors should be prepared. Specifically, we believe that graduate students should begin to develop professional competence in the major responsibilities that faculty members actually have, namely teaching, research, and professional service; have learning experiences in the different settings in which the profession is practiced, e.g., colleges and universities with different missions, student bodies, and faculty responsibilities; and learn about the complexities of teaching and service in course work, workshops, and seminars, and by working with mentors in teaching and professional service.

This report analyzes PFF programs that have involved nearly three dozen major universities that award large numbers of doctoral degrees. Phase I graduate universities each formed a "cluster" of diverse institutions into partnerships that provided doctoral students direct experience in two or more different kinds of institutions. Phase II involves fifteen doctoral universities and ninety-three partner institutions. Phase III adds eleven doctoral universities and twenty-six partner institutions. (The complete list of institutions can be found in the Appendix.) Phase IV is in the process of conducting a competition that will add still more clusters.

The last five years might be viewed as a "demonstration project" for PFF ideas and practices that, we conclude, are a practical way to improve on traditional doctoral programs as preparation for an academic career. Although this is a report on a work very much in progress as PFF initiatives continue to be refined, we believe it is time to share the lessons that we have learned with all who play some role in the graduate preparation of the professoriate. The main lesson is that we can, and should, incorporate PFF ideas and practices into graduate study for students interested in an academic career.

The PFF program has found that:

◆ Graduate students are enthusiastic about the opportunities to learn about the complexities of teaching and service and to begin integrating them with their ability to conduct research;

◆ Faculty members who serve as mentors gain renewed vitality and professional development from working with advanced graduate students; and

◆ Almost all those associated with PFF programs believe they are more effective than traditional programs, that they are not very costly, and that they can be replicated.

The primary audience we are addressing are those who think that the graduate education of future academics should be changed to include more emphasis on preparation for teaching, for service, and for understanding faculty responsibilities in diverse institutions. This audience includes graduate deans, department chairs, graduate student advisors in academic departments, graduate faculty members, and staff members in graduate teaching assistant development programs. At the approximately 3,500 U.S. institutions seeking to hire new faculty members who are prepared to make contributions immediately, this group includes presidents, academic administrators, department chairs, and faculty members. Chairs and members of search committees for new faculty members should be especially interested in a growing pool of candidates that have received special preparation for their future responsibilities. In addition, graduate students will find that this volume speaks to some of their most serious concerns about the adequacy of their preparation. State policy makers, government leaders, graduate fellowship administrators, researchers studying higher education, and others who care about the quality and future of American higher education will find much that is germane to their roles.

The initiative analyzed here is but one of many that, together, mark an academy in transition. Research universities, especially, are the focus of efforts to change academic practices. Related initiatives are broadening the definitions of scholarship and its assessment (Boyer 1990; Rice 1991; and Glassick, Huber, and Maeroff 1997), changing the reward structure (Diamond and Adams 1993), redefining faculty roles (Rice 1996), encouraging post-tenure review (Licatta 1998), emphasizing teaching and learning (Shulman and Hutchings 1998), increasing faculty diversity (Abraham, Pepion, and Moody 1994), supporting graduate teaching assistants (Marincovich, Prostko, and Stout 1998), and enhancing undergraduate education (Kenny, et al. 1998). We understand that it does little good to give special preparation to graduate students if they enter a profession that neglects professionalism in teaching and service and if they enter institutions that do not value their broader expertise. Enhanced graduate preparation goes hand in glove with these other initiatives to redefine faculty work and, ultimately, improve the quality of education for all students.

We do not know what the academy in general or the research university in particular will look like after this transition is complete, but we have no doubt that it will be different from what it is today. We hope that the preparation of future faculty described in this volume will become the norm.

Writing This Report

The writing of this report was a truly collaborative process. The start can be traced to a national conference for PFF in the summer of 1995. A group of individuals, The Writing Committee, was asked to organize itself so that someone could attend each session, capture the best ideas, and report on them in the final session. That worked so well that we repeated the process in the conference in 1996 and asked the group to follow up with a written statement that would form the basis of a report. The group, chaired by James Slevin, professor of English at Georgetown University and a consultant to PFF, included:

Leigh DeNeef, professor of English and associate dean, Graduate School, Duke University

Stuart Noble-Goodman, then a graduate student in English and PFF participant, Duke University

Zoe Irvin, chair of mathematics, Howard Community College

Ricki Shine, coordinator, Honors Program, Northeastern Illinois University

Jan Smith, program director, Preparing Future Faculty, Office of Human Resources, University of Minnesota

Louis J. Swift, associate vice chancellor and dean of undergraduate studies, University of Kentucky

Orlando Taylor, professor of communication and dean of the Graduate School of Arts and Sciences, Howard University

When the pieces came in, the chair edited them for coherence. The manuscript remained unfinished until now, when the central staff of PFF was able to expand on the work of the writing committee and draft the current report. After reviews by coordinators of each cluster and several revisions, the manuscript was edited and produced by AAC&U and CGS staff.

Organization of this Report

Chapter One offers a new vision of graduate preparation for college and university professors, presents the ideas underlying PFF programs, and describes four phases in the development of the PFF program. As with any new approach, some features are unfamiliar or require special attention, so that in Chapter Two we identify three such features and explain how PFF attempts to deal with them. Chapter Three describes the experiences of graduate students, often in their own words, and illustrates both the benefits and difficulties of their participation. Chapter Four analyzes the challenges of sustaining PFF programs, addressing inclusiveness and, ultimately, changing the "culture of preparation." The concluding chapter offers a practical strategy for institutional change that responds to calls for doctoral study of future faculty to emphasize a balance of instruction in research, teaching, and service and focuses on the needs of the institutions that employ Ph.D.s. Action recommendations are directed to graduate students, faculty, administrators, leaders from institutions that hire faculty, learned societies, and fellowship funders. Lists of participating PFF institutions are found in the Appendix, along with additional materials and resources.

Acknowledgments

This volume literally could not have been written without the hard work of the people in the clusters. They devised the innovative PFF programs, learned a great deal in the process, shared their insights—both positive and negative—with us, wrote informative materials, and critiqued our ideas. The graduate deans who were the principal investigators, the cluster coordinators who administered the PFF programs on a day-to-day basis, and the graduate student coordinators at many places have pioneered these new approaches and taught us a great deal about how well they work. Chairs and other leaders of PFF in departments, academic administrators, faculty mentors in "partner" institutions, and, of course, hundreds of graduate students themselves: all deserve our heartfelt appreciation for their pioneering efforts and for helping to inform us about what they were doing and accomplishing.

We also want to acknowledge the constant support we have received from the presidents of our two associations, Jules B. LaPidus, president of the Council of Graduate Schools, and Paula P. Brownlee, president of the Association of

American Colleges and Universities until her retirement in January 1998, and Carol Geary Schneider, her successor. Each has been a strong supporter of our work and made possible an extraordinarily effective collaboration between these two associations, a feat that, unfortunately, is rare in this city.

Two other individuals have made substantial contributions to the success of the PFF program by serving as extensions of the staff: Howard Anderson, emeritus professor of English and former associate dean of the Graduate School at Michigan State University, and James Slevin, professor of English at Georgetown University. Howard was dean in residence at the Council of Graduate Schools when the first grant was received, and he helped write materials for the first competition and other communications. He and Jim traveled to many of the clusters, listening to both successes and struggles and offering valuable advice to leaders trying to give birth to vibrant new programs in the face of skeptical colleagues. They also led sessions at PFF meetings and conferences and gave valuable advice to the staff throughout the effort, including the preparation of this report.

We want to extend a special note of appreciation to our funders. The Pew Charitable Trusts provided more than six years of support to launch the PFF program. Throughout the entire program, Ellen Wert, our program officer at Pew, has been as supportive as any foundation officer ever could be, often pitching in to make plans, conduct meetings, moderate sessions at professional meetings and other activities. Russell Edgerton, director of education for the Trusts, like his predecessor, Robert Schwartz, provided valuable leadership to make this effort possible. The National Science Foundation, too, has provided generous support, and Myles Boylan, our program officer, has given wise advice and helped PFF to create a presence in the science community. We hope this report justifies the substantial investment, personal as well as financial, of these friends and foundations in this effort.

Iris Jacobs provided very able clerical and technological support in the PFF program and in preparing this report. Bridget Puzon, AAC&U's academic editor, provided valuable assistance in the final stages of this report.

JERRY G. GAFF, *vice president for education and institutional renewal at AAC&U and director, Preparing Future Faculty*

ANNE S. PRUITT-LOGAN, *scholar in residence at CGS and co-director, Preparing Future Faculty*

RICHARD A. WEIBL, *director of programs for education and institutional renewal at AAC&U and program manager, Preparing Future Faculty*

Washington, D.C.
January 2000

CHAPTER 1

A New Vision for Preparing Future Faculty

This volume is a call to change the ways we educate future college professors and a guide for developing the programs to do it. The changes we propose should in no way be seen as replacing the research training that is the heart of doctoral study. Rather, we intend to broaden the concept of academic professionalism—currently defined largely by research—by including preparation for teaching and for service. By *teaching* we mean preparing courses, developing syllabi, and designing curricula for educational programs both within one's field and across the institution; managing classroom learning; defining learning experiences beyond classrooms; using appropriate technology; serving as mentor; and assessing learning. By *service* we mean sharing in the governance of academic units and institutions and contributing to professional associations and communities. Each of these areas has a body of scholarship and a set of values, norms, and expectations of faculty members that is shaped by the missions and heritages of different educational settings. This broader definition of academic professionalism significantly enriches the education of aspiring faculty members. It requires expanding the educational resources beyond graduate faculty members in research universities to include individuals and resources from other types of colleges and universities.

We should be clear that the goal of PFF is to prepare students for the full range of faculty responsibilities. Just as some (mistakenly) think that this broader education must de-value research, others (mistakenly) regard it solely as a teaching initiative. PFF is not a glorified teaching assistant program. The goal is to prepare future assistant professors who have already begun to develop professional competence in teaching, research, and professional service. Throughout this manuscript, we refer to this full set of roles when we use terms like college or university professor or teacher, unless otherwise specified.

The changes we urge provide vastly more sophisticated preparation for aspiring faculty members so that they are ready to make a quick and sure start in the faculty positions they attain. We think that graduate students interested in an academic career should learn the basics of these matters and begin learning to integrate the demands of teaching, research, and service. We believe that these proposals constitute a win-win-win strategy: better preparation for the graduate students, better faculty candidates for the colleges and universities that hire them, and stronger and more engaging programs for graduate schools and departments. Ultimately, we expect that this new preparation will result in better education for undergraduate *and* graduate students.

These are not unrealistic, blue sky recommendations. They are practical ideas that, under the rubric of Preparing Future Faculty (PFF), have guided innovative programs for several years in nearly three dozen leading universities in the United States. We have learned that PFF programs are more robust approaches to faculty preparation than conventional ones.

How Did We Get to Where We Are?
How Do We Get Beyond It?

Until the late 19th century, before the doctoral research degree was imported to the United States, professional standards for college faculty were nonexistent. Most colleges at the time were sponsored by religious bodies, and character and religious belief were primary qualifications for faculty. It was then that leading American educators discovered the power of German universities that were based on research and scientific discovery; the focus on research gave them an opportunity to develop professional academic standards based on the process of inquiry and the advance of knowledge. Universities like Johns Hopkins embraced the idea that professors should be scholars in their disciplines, and they developed an advanced research degree: the Doctor of Philosophy. Doctoral education came to be defined as study of a specialization within one of the academic disciplines, small seminars on central aspects of the field as well as courses on cutting edge research, a qualifying examination to determine readiness to do independent research, apprenticeship to a research mentor, and original research in the form of a dissertation. Gradually, this experience was deemed necessary for most university and college faculty.

Although this 19th century model is now widespread, we believe that it is inadequate for the challenges confronting the professoriate of the 21st century. The ability to conduct research is a necessary but not sufficient condition for the roles of the vast majority of college professors. Just as doctoral education earlier was transformed by the idea that faculty must possess expert knowledge of their field and be able to conduct original research, so is preparation changing again in light of today's need for faculty who are not only able researchers but also effective teachers and leaders of their profession. We must articulate broader and more comprehensive definitions of professionalism among faculty members—and prepare future generations to attain them. Several problems with the conventional approach can be identified.

> *We must articulate broader and more comprehensive definitions of professionalism among faculty members—and prepare future generations to attain them.*

1. A mismatch exists between doctoral education and the needs of colleges and universities that employ new Ph.D.s. One hundred and two universities—primarily research universities—award 80 percent of doctorates (Gaff and Lambert 1996). Students who aspire to faculty careers are routinely socialized to the values of academic life in universities like these. Those who go on to faculty careers, however, work mostly in thousands of other institutions that have different missions, student bodies, and expectations for faculty. We believe that academic leaders should work to broaden the context of socialization to include the culture of institutions that hire new faculty.

One manifestation of this disconnect is evident in the growth in the numbers of Ph.D.s earned and the lack of comparable growth in positions with the major employers of individuals with doctorates. A total of 42,705 individuals were awarded doctorates in 1997 (National Research Council 1998), an increase of nearly one-third from a decade earlier. Many of the graduates seek faculty positions in vain. A large part of the reason for this state of affairs is the expansion of doctoral programs for reasons that have little to do with the need for the graduates. Faculty conduct research to enhance scholarship as well as their reputations, administrations seek stronger graduate programs and national rankings, and government keeps supporting research—all of which require graduate students to achieve these aims. At the same time, colleges and universities are reducing the number of full-time faculty positions and replacing them with part-time or temporary faculty as a way to reduce the cost of instructional programs.

Another manifestation of the disconnect between the kind of education provided and the kind of work expected of faculty members can be seen in faculty searches. Institutions conducting searches for faculty in most fields routinely receive hundreds of applications, but faculty members and administrators at hiring institutions tell us that most applicants provide no evidence of expertise in teaching, awareness of the special qualities of that institution, or expectations that they will contribute to departmental or institutional initiatives. The difficult job market for new Ph.D.s may be the result of inadequate preparation for the jobs that exist.

This mismatch has influenced the leaders of several learned societies to call for significant change in doctoral education. The Committee on Professional Employment of the Modern Language Association (1997) laments "Many doctoral students have been acculturated to define themselves as failures if they do not land jobs exactly like those of their professors" (p. 23). The report recommends that "doctoral programs offer courses on pedagogy"; familiarize students "with the complex system of postsecondary and secondary education in this country"; and offer not just courses but also "mentored internships, residencies, and exchanges among institutions" (p. 32). Similarly, the Presidential Task Force of the American Chemical Society (1995) concluded that departments of chemistry should sponsor "appropriate forums for students to learn about teaching in four-year and two-year colleges" (p. 18).

Doctoral education has erred by focusing almost exclusively on the cutting edge issues of concern to the disciplines and ignoring the uses to which its degrees are being put. It has sought to create more researchers who can advance knowledge of the field, while ignoring the consequences of its programs.

We believe that graduate education should adopt the basic tenet of American pragmatism and focus *also* on the consequences of its programs, on the actual work done by those with doctoral degrees, and on how well traditional programs prepare them for it.

2. Graduate schools and departments seldom gather data with which to assess their programs. Without reliable information, leaders are unable to track the careers of their graduates to determine how their programs could better prepare graduates for the realities of professional employment. The Ohio Board of Regents (OBOR), as part of a review of all graduate programs in the state, required an employment survey of graduates. During a site visit to a participating PFF campus, one of the authors asked faculty members in one department "Do you know where your graduates are?" Delighted to say yes, because the department had just completed its OBOR survey, a faculty member mentioned several alumni who were in prestigious positions, and—almost as an afterthought—one alumnus employed at a small liberal arts college in the state. The OBOR survey uncovered many situations like this: other than in prestigious institutions, no one in the department knew where the others were or how they happened to get there. Such data are indispensable to understanding the actual careers of graduates in order to more closely align doctoral education with the needs of colleges and universities employing the graduates.

3. The academy has resources that might be mobilized to preparing the future professoriate. The preparation of prospective faculty members takes virtually no advantage of the opportunity to provide them with the kinds of apprenticeships that other professions provide as a matter of course. Medical students, from the earliest days of matriculation, work on hospital floors and in a variety of clinics, later serving as interns and residents with increased responsibilities. Law students work in clinical courses, and others are interns in firms or with justices practicing the legal work they aspire to do. Business students, from their undergraduate years, are immersed in the worlds of work that they train to enter. Seminarians, while still on the way to their degrees, work in parishes, preach, and minister in centers for the poor and infirm. In professions like these, teaching and learning is understood to occur experientially at many sites and to be conducted by many professionals other than those commissioned by degree programs to conduct courses. This is more than a plea for experiential learning, as valuable as that may be. It is a fundamental matter of understanding that the entire profession can and should play a role in the preparation and renewal of its members.

It is ironic—and unfortunate—that higher education so oddly restricts its professional preparation to the classrooms and laboratories of research universities. Regrettably, faculties in other settings—liberal arts colleges, comprehensive universities, community colleges—are not involved. A graduate student in one of the new Preparing Future Faculty programs eloquently expressed this idea:

> My graduate mentor was the best teacher I ever had. That is not common, I know, but it's true, and I think it makes me aware of what PFF is really about. We are not "dissing" graduate faculty as scholarly slugs indifferent to their roles as educators; as I say, my mentor cared deeply about his students and about teaching, and was great at it. It's just that he didn't have a clue about anything outside our classroom, including the kind of career I actually envisioned for myself and the kind of institution I wanted to hire me. He was a generous man who taught me everything I needed to know about literary theory and

eighteenth-century literature and how I might go about producing important knowledge in these fields; he also showed me some nifty ways of teaching a graduate seminar to people like myself. That's very important stuff. But there is so much more, and I don't even fault him for not knowing about it. I fault the system that made him my only mentor.

The research university, as a context, necessarily limits, narrows, and, frankly, mis-educates graduate students for the realities of academic life elsewhere. It is unwise and wasteful to regard faculties in other settings as less capable professionals. We believe that a more inclusive and comprehensive model of professional preparation is preferable.

4. Changes taking place in faculty roles and in higher education tend not to be reflected in doctoral preparation. Many leaders of doctoral education are not even aware of these changes. Below are a few common changes:

a. Excellent teaching is coming to be expected by employing institutions. Faculty searches are attracting large numbers of applicants, and search committees are able to concentrate their attention on those applicants with teaching experience and with evidence of effectiveness. Graduate students who lack teaching experience, supervision and support from faculty members, expertise with some of the newer technological, collaborative, and experiential approaches to teaching and learning, and evidence of success, are at a disadvantage.

Further, we are seeing a shift from teaching to learning that requires dramatic changes in student-faculty interaction (Bar and Tag 1995). Increasingly, faculty are expected to do more than simply cover the content of their fields; they are expected to be more intentional in fostering student learning. This means developing specific goals for student learning, using a variety of methods to cultivate learning, and assessing learning. Faculty are expected to effectively relate to and teach students from many cultures, with a wide range of learning styles, interests, and levels of ability; new instructional demands are placed on faculty.

b. Faculty today must be able to work not just independently but also collaboratively. Increasingly, faculty must work with colleagues to foster program coherence and assure the achievement of valued learning goals although their experiences as researchers, especially in the humanities and social sciences, is mainly solitary and often competitive. Productive collaborative skills can be learned. Specialists must understand how an educational program as a whole contributes to the overall growth of students. These qualities should be acquired by aspiring faculty members. Only an occasional doctoral program prepares students for these demands.

c. *Faculty members are expected to render service to their departments and institutions—to be campus and community citizens who actively participate in governing their institutions.* Professional service and shared governance should be honored and rewarded, both in preparation programs and in faculty life. And these involve such things as setting shared goals, conducting strategic planning, making important personnel decisions about hiring or promoting colleagues, raising funds, creating and monitoring budgets, relating to the public, and conducting program reviews. Too often, new faculty are being hired with the expectation that they can make such important contributions from the time they set foot on the campus.

d. *Respect for the professionalism surrounding the complex of activities that are bundled under the rubrics of "teaching" and "service" is needed.* During their doctoral studies few faculty members are informed of the significant research and professional literature that exists on teaching, learning, the curriculum, and the administration and organization of colleges and universities. Indeed, often this literature is disparaged, and doctoral students and new faculty are discouraged from exploring it mainly by scholars who themselves are unfamiliar with it. Rather than discouraging students from discussing teaching, learning, curriculum, assessment, and institutional support for professional work, for instance, we believe that doctoral programs should deliberately cultivate such study and discussion.

It is timely to develop doctoral programs that address the mismatch with hiring institutions and that address changing responsibilities of faculty members. The academic workforce, in the midst of a major transition, is larger and includes a greater variety of individuals than often realized. Finkelstein, Seal, and Schuster (1998) found in 1992–1993 that the number of faculty in the academic labor force was 1,033,966. Of this number, 435,735 were part-time faculty. Although these data are the last national information available, most observers believe that this number is increasing. An additional 83,255 were "non-core" faculty such as nonteaching professionals, librarians, and counselors, who have faculty status. A "core" of 514,976 were full-time teaching faculty. Another factor to consider is age. Over one-third of those who work in four- and two-year schools are over 55 years of age. Moreover, some junior and mid-career faculty leave their positions each year. It is likely that as many as 40 percent of the core faculty will be replaced in the next decade. All of these factors will create a significant change in the composition of the faculty ranks. Now, when large numbers of graduate students are in the pipeline preparing to join the professoriate and when large numbers of openings are becoming available, it is time for new approaches to be implemented.

Nationally, the impact of these changes can already be seen at the campus level. A liberal arts Roman Catholic college in Pennsylvania has replaced about half of its faculty in the last six years. At a community college in southern California nearly a quarter of its faculty are new, and in its three-campus district, 45 percent of the faculty are eligible for retirement. At a nontraditional institution in New York that serves working adults, 60 percent of its faculty are expected to retire in ten years. In addition, a number of new state universities are being created: Florida Gulf Coast University, California State University at San Marcos, and Arizona State University both West and East campuses, are all hiring new faculty. Academics know that even a single new faculty member can make a big difference in the character of education in a small department, and two or three can cause a sea change in larger departments. The potential impact of the generational change on many individual campuses is hard to overstate.

> The changing of the guard is an excellent opportunity to alter traditional ways of doing things, but unless the new faculty are prepared differently than their professors were, it will be an opportunity lost.

Donald Kennedy (1997) argues that significant change in academic practices is needed and that it will be led by new faculty members fresh out of their graduate studies. The changing of the guard is an excellent opportunity to alter traditional ways of doing things, but unless the new faculty are prepared differently than their professors were, it will be an opportunity lost. We believe that there should be a sense of urgency to alter graduate programs now so that they create a different future for the next generation of faculty members.

One other factor suggests it is timely to make innovations in doctoral preparation programs—the poor job market for academics in virtually all fields, at least from the perspective of candidates and the institutions producing them. From the perspective of those *hiring*, however, the job market is excellent. Institutions now have the power to choose new faculty who meet *their* specific needs. Colleges and universities have been able to raise their hiring standards and to demand of candidates not only research expertise but also a track record as a teacher and the ability to serve the department and the institution. Graduates with doctoral degrees based exclusively on traditional research competencies—even from outstanding departments at leading universities—are no longer as competitive as they once were. The academic job market, then, is favorable to the creation of new kinds of preparation programs.

In summary, it is time to face the shortcomings of conventional ways of preparing college professors and to develop ways that reflect contemporary expectations of professional academics. Colleges and universities are defining new professional standards for faculty that call for higher, more comprehensive, more inclusive, and more competent performance. Needed are doctoral programs that help those interested in an academic career to understand those new professional standards and to begin a lifelong practice of learning excellence in teaching, research, and service.

Basic Ideas

Preparing Future Faculty (PFF) is one of a number of new approaches based on the principle that graduate education can and should acquaint those students aspiring to academic careers with the broad and complex realities of faculty life. It is an effort to transform the way aspiring faculty members are prepared for their careers, moving toward an education that is informed by the kinds of responsibilities faculty members actually have in a variety of institutions.

PFF is both a *configuration of ideas* and a *national program*. It is built on a spirit of *partnership and cooperation* that yields a more comprehensive model for preparing the future professoriate.

The *configuration of ideas* underlying PFF can be easily described. For most graduate students moving into an academic career, their professional lives will entail not only teaching their discipline but also teaching, through their discipline, the habits of mind characteristic of a liberal education. It will also involve making a difficult transition from, for example, being a chemist with a specialty to being a chemist who works within an institution with a specific mission, norms, and expectations—and who continues to maintain a disciplinary specialization and identity.

The most general idea is that the doctoral experience should include a) increasingly independent and varied teaching responsibilities, b) opportunities to grow and develop as a researcher, and c) opportunities to serve the department and campus. More specific ideas include the following:

1. Apprenticeship teaching, research, and service experiences should be planned so that they are appropriate to the student's stage of personal development and progress toward the degree. Doctoral students assigned as teaching assistants, for example, tend to be viewed as "covering a course section" rather than developing professional expertise benefitting themselves and students. Future faculty should be given progressively more complex assignments, more responsibility and recognition associated with increased professional capacities.

2. Doctoral students should learn about the academic profession through exposure to the range of professional responsibilities in the variety of institutions that may become their professional homes. Becoming aware of the

variety of institutions enables them to find a better "fit" between their own interests and competencies and the needs of institutions.

3. Doctoral programs should include a formalized system for mentoring in all aspects of professional development. Just as students have a mentor to guide their research, they also need guidance as they develop their teaching and service repertoire. Indeed, a student can benefit from multiple mentors. A teaching mentor may be at a different institution, perhaps one with a mission that is distinctively different than is usual in research universities.

4. Doctoral experiences should equip future faculty for the changes taking place in teaching and classrooms. For example, future faculty will have to be competent in using technology and addressing issues presented by increasing heterogeneity among students, and they should be sophisticated about using the newer, active, collaborative, technological, and experiential approaches to teaching and learning.

5. Professional development experiences should be thoughtfully integrated into the academic program and sequence of degree requirements. Unless leaders of doctoral education are intentional about these matters and structure these new experiences into their programs, PFF activities are likely to be haphazard. Careful integration can avoid lengthening time to degree.

6. Where high-quality teaching assistant orientation and development programs are available, PFF programs should build upon them. PFF is consistent with the best practices of teaching assistant development, while also advancing another, more comprehensive level of preparation. While teaching assistant development programs are valuable in supporting certain faculty roles, PFF programs broaden the preparation by including teaching experience at different institutions, providing mentors for information and feedback, and stressing professional service and governance responsibilities of various sorts.

None of these ideas is new or radical, but collectively they add up to a very different kind of doctoral experience than has been conventional.

PFF as a National Program: Phase I, 1993–1996

As a national program consisting of four related initiatives, PFF is an activity of the Association of American Colleges and Universities and the Council of Graduate Schools. Phases I and II were supported by The Pew Charitable Trusts. In the first phase of this program, grants totaling about $1 million were awarded to seventeen research universities to develop models of more effective ways to prepare doctoral students for the professoriate. One of the stipulations was that each research university would assemble a cluster of diverse institutions and work as partners to decide together the kind of doctoral preparation that is needed, and then they would provide opportunities for doctoral students to get personal experience with faculty life on diverse campuses. The idea was to bring the "consumers" of Ph.D.s together with the "producers" and thereby develop programs that are more nearly suited to the needs of hiring institutions. Altogether, the seventeen original participating universities worked with sixty-eight partner institutions, a group that included nine members of the Association of American Universities, eleven land grant universities, thirteen community colleges, eight historically black colleges and universities, six women's colleges, and scores of liberal arts and comprehensive institutions. (A list may be found in the Appendix.) It was a rich mix that reflected the diversity of American higher education.

PHASES OF THE PREPARING FUTURE FACULTY PROGRAM

Dates	Purposes	Funder	Participants
1993–1997	Develop model programs	The Pew Charitable Trusts	17 clusters
1997–2000	Institutionalize and spread programs	The Pew Charitable Trusts	15 clusters
1998–2000	Develop model programs in the sciences and mathematics	National Science Foundation	20 departments & clusters
1999–2002	Develop model programs in the humanities and social sciences	A private gift	24 departments & clusters

The configuration of ideas underlying PFF guided the establishment of new programs within the clusters. Since each cluster was encouraged to tailor its program to local needs and circumstances, no typical program can be described. Nonetheless, the flavor of programs can be gained by illustrative activities in three domains.

Universities, for example, offered courses on college teaching and learning, held forums on faculty life and careers, and helped doctoral students prepare portfolios documenting their expertise in teaching, research, and service.

Departments offered courses on the teaching of their subject, provided sequences of supervised teaching experiences, and held forums for faculty members at different institutions to discuss their professional histories, career paths, and life styles.

Partner institutions assigned teaching mentors to work with doctoral students, offered supervised teaching opportunities, invited students to attend departmental or faculty meetings, and included doctoral students in faculty development activities.

Although programs varied, all incorporated a broader and more comprehensive vision of doctoral preparation for aspiring faculty than has been tradition, and all provided students with experience in institutions markedly different from their own universities.

Structures of PFF Clusters

Since the clusters of institutions were encouraged to develop a variety of model programs that reflected their own institutional strengths, needs, and opportunities, it is not surprising that they developed different structures.

◆ At some clusters, PFF utilizes a centralized approach. The University of Minnesota, for instance, built upon a well-defined, centralized, teaching assistant development program, bridging outward to local cluster campuses and, where possible, linking with departmental initiatives. Howard University took advantage of the PFF initiative to establish a more comprehensive central teaching assistant program that was integrally linked to the PFF program. Arizona State University located its leadership in the Graduate College and also is taking steps to encourage and coordinate departmentally based activities.

◆ At other clusters, PFF is developed around coordinated departmental initiatives. Although the departments devise their own distinctive programs, central university offices, such as the graduate school or instructional development program, provide a sense of shared purpose and frequent opportunities to cross-fertilize. Florida State University, Indiana University, and the University of Washington exemplify this approach.

◆ At still other clusters, PFF is connected with programs for faculty development, working outward to incorporate doctoral students as aspiring faculty and faculty colleagues on the cluster campuses. Teaching and learning centers are primarily responsible for staffing the programs at the Universities of Kentucky and Wisconsin-Milwaukee.

◆ At some clusters PFF finds its center of gravity in a single department, where energetic and innovative leadership has integrated doctoral preparation and the incorporation of local colleagues to show the way to more comprehensive, multi-departmental, and institutional change. Such is the case of the department of mathematics at Cornell University.

♦ Some clusters include as many as eleven partner institutions, while others have as few as four. In most cases, the partners are in close proximity to minimize time and logistical problems associated with transportation, but a few universities, such as the Universities of Nebraska and New Hampshire, have established relationships with partners far away through distance learning arrangements.

The spirit of partnership and cooperation evident at each cluster has also marked the national program, instilling it with a sense of mutual learning and growth.

This variety of models is a strength of PFF. As a national program, PFF has flourished from this diversity, allowing leaders of each cluster to learn from the others. Indeed, the spirit of partnership and cooperation evident at each cluster has also marked the national program, instilling it with a sense of mutual learning and growth.

We have conducted extensive assessments of the PFF programs, with some of the results discussed in the next two chapters. Suffice it to say here that the early evidence from multiple sources—faculty members in doctoral universities and in partner institutions, graduate students, and administrators—confirms the value of these programs.

Preparing Future Faculty: Phase II, 1997–2000

During the first three years of PFF, far more was accomplished than any of us expected. Our experience and assessments during this project convinced us that a second phase of PFF could build on the initial achievements and reach two further goals: a) deepen and extend current programs within the institutions, and b) propagate PFF programs to other sites by spreading the lessons learned throughout academe.

A second phase was funded by The Pew Charitable Trusts to carry the program into the next century. The primary purpose of Phase Two is to move from a demonstration project to a new way of conducting doctoral education, from a pilot project to institutionalizing this approach. Another competitive application process resulted in a selection of ten clusters from among the original seventeen. All institutions maintained the programs with their own funding during the intervening year between the two phases; in fact, most expanded the programs because they saw the power of PFF programs. For instance, Florida

State University's program expanded from four to ten departments. Similar growth was experienced at Arizona State, Howard, and most other universities involved.

In a parallel competition among universities that had developed similar but independent programs with their own funding, five were invited to join the program. Indiana University launched its own initiative when the dean of the Graduate School offered three-year start-up grants for departments to experiment with PFF ideas and programs. If, after three years, a department finds the results valuable, it must provide funding to continue its program. Thus, several different models exist, and the Graduate School is developing mechanisms to bring participants together around common agendas.

Syracuse University developed a Future Professoriate Project as part of its massive effort to emphasize undergraduate education in reshaping itself as a "student-centered research university." It identified a number of faculty members willing to become teaching mentors, created an advanced position for doctoral students to be graduate teaching *associates* with more responsibilities and higher pay than graduate teaching *assistants*, helped students develop teaching portfolios, and awarded a Certificate in College Teaching.

The University of Colorado operated an exemplary teaching assistant development program. In the process, they trained forty lead graduate teaching assistants to work with their peers and faculty in their own departments to hold colloquia on teaching-related issues and to support departmental teaching assistants. They are piggy-backing the PFF program onto this existing effort.

The University of Nebraska also operated a teaching assistant program. They wanted to take advantage of their state-of-the-art distance learning facility and staff to experiment with institutional partnerships not in the locality. Leadership by senior professors, not administrators or staff, gives it a distinctive flavor.

The University of New Hampshire developed programs in college teaching that could be added to its doctoral programs. A 12-credit cognate is available for students in any department, and students wanting a more substantial learning experience can earn a master's degree in college teaching. This strategy allows students to enrich their doctoral studies without the need to alter any existing programs.

All fifteen universities assembled clusters to institutionalize and propagate such programs in other settings. Currently, a total of 108 diverse institutions are involved in this work, and in general, they, too, are expanding their programs.

Preparing Future Science and Mathematics Faculty: Phase III, 1998–2001

With support from the National Science Foundation a third program has been launched for infusing PFF ideas and programs into academic disciplines in the sciences and mathematics. We have developed partnerships with the American Association of Physics Teachers, American Chemical Society, Special Interest Group on Computer Science Education of the Association for Computing Machinery, and both the American Mathematical Society and Mathematical Association of America working together.

The professional societies have selected doctoral degree-granting departments to receive grants to create—over a two-year period—innovative programs based on PFF ideas. The societies intend to monitor and assess the progress of these programs and highlight promising practices at their meetings, in publications, and electronic communications. The expectation is that by infusing these innovative ideas through the professional societies and securing leadership for PFF programs from respected faculty members, they will become the rule rather than the exception in doctoral education.

Preparing Future Social Science and Humanities Faculty: Phase IV, 1999–2002

We recently received word about support for a fourth phase. This effort parallels the initiative in the sciences and mathematics and involves learned societies in six humanities and social science disciplines. The societies involved are the American Historical Association, American Political Science Association, American Psychological Association, American Sociological Association, National Council of Teachers of English, and National Communication Association. Each society is conducting a national competition to select up to four departments to develop model PFF programs and highlight their progress in their publications and programs.

Other Faculty Preparation Programs

As PFF ideas were becoming widely known and accepted and the national program was developing, several other universities not formally associated with the national program established their own versions of faculty preparation programs.

Similar programs have been developed at institutions as diverse as Louisville University, the University of Arkansas, University of California at Davis and at Irvine, University of Michigan, University of Utah, and Wayne State University, among others. The University of South Carolina has developed a new program, Preparing Future African American Faculty. Seeking both to increase the number of African American faculty members and give them more effective preparation for college teaching, this program provides doctoral students with the opportunity to teach, receive assistance from a supervising faculty member on teaching approaches, and develop a more comprehensive professional portfolio.

From the growth of interest in these new approaches, it appears that something fundamental is taking place, and that it transcends the work of a single funded program. Whatever is pressing for new approaches also transcends the borders of the United States. We have been in contact with leaders of similar programs in other countries as diverse as Austria, Brazil, Canada, England, France, and India.

New faculty preparation programs have come a long way, and we have learned a lot. But if we are to succeed in changing the culture surrounding the preparation of future faculty members, we have much farther to go. The progress made and the enthusiasm of those involved in these new programs encourage us to push ahead. We believe that we have found a better way, and a growing number of like-minded colleagues are joining in this endeavor.

CHAPTER 2

Three Critical Elements in Establishing Preparing Future Faculty Programs

A ny innovative program faces a number of challenges as its leaders test ideas in practice, assess results, and, if successful, incorporate the program into the life of the institution. Leaders of new programs implicitly threaten the existing order. Traditional practices are in place precisely because they work more or less well, and, as a consequence, they have defenders. In addition, advocates encounter skeptics or critics, many of whom are unaware of the problems created by current practices and uninformed of new approaches. In this section we identify three critical issues in the establishment of new faculty preparation programs and discuss how we seek to deal with them: establishing new institutional partnerships, developing new forms of mentoring, and understanding the centrality of the faculty.

The Clusters: New Institutional Partnerships

The vision sketched in Chapter One involves new kinds of inter-institutional relationships. Colleges and universities as independent corporate entities in a market-based economy compete with each other—for students, faculty, tuition, support from the state, gifts from donors, grants, favorable publicity, even athletic superiority. In short, they compete for anything that will advance themselves ahead of the others. One of the ways institutions compete is among a number of hierarchies in which prestige is accorded to those higher in the accepted pecking order. In this context individuals associated with different institutions tend to be suspicious of each other, jealously guarding their own prerogatives and resources, and sensitive to perceived slights. PFF challenges this dynamic by creating collaborative institutional relationships.

Resistance to such collaboration is a common response when one first hears about PFF. Graduate faculty and deans often ask why they need to involve undergraduate institutions in what has been their exclusive province. We believe that graduate universities, by themselves, cannot fully prepare doctoral students for faculty responsibilities in other kinds of institutions. Moreover, few of the graduate faculty have ever worked in liberal arts colleges, comprehensive universities, or community colleges, the very kinds of institutions that hire the bulk of academics. Many graduate faculty are not as aware of faculty responsibilities at institutions focused on undergraduate education. They also tend to be removed from the realities of the current job market for faculty. Predominantly undergraduate institutions offer faculty viewpoints and venues that can inform and enrich the work of doctoral education.

> **P**redominantly *undergraduate institutions offer faculty viewpoints and venues that can inform and enrich the work of doctoral education.*

On the other hand, faculty and deans at predominantly undergraduate institutions often ask, "Why would we want to help the university with its doctoral programs? What's in it for us?" The answers are multiple. Part of it is the discontent with the quality of preparation presented by candidates for assistant professor positions. Moreover, almost every professor has bad memories about how s/he was simply thrown into the classroom, had to learn to teach on his or her own, and the unfortunate mistakes made as a young faculty member. Many want to help other neophytes start their careers with more support. But it is not all altruism. Few of these faculty ever have the opportunity to work with advanced doctoral students, and they value the professional stimulation and personal vitality gained from working with them and the graduate faculty. The new partnerships bring benefits to both sides, benefits that require a new spirit of collaboration and equality.

To abandon the old competitive hierarchy and adopt a more collaborative approach, new ways of thinking are needed. One of the most important lessons we have learned is this: *PFF thrives on institutional collaboration and falters in its absence*. Instituting PFF thus requires commitment to a collaborative process, involving trust and respect among all the constituencies that benefit from the success of the program.

Forming a Cluster. Because a variety of immersion experiences for doctoral students helps to focus fundamental questions about institutional missions and the multiple and complex responsibilities of faculty members, decisions about the composition of the cluster are therefore important. Typically, PFF clusters include comprehensive universities, community colleges, liberal arts colleges, and even (at two current sites) another research university, thereby providing PFF students experience at a different type of university. Across these categories, the PFF commitment to provide diverse experiences has led clusters to look toward religious schools, historically black institutions, women's colleges, tribal colleges, and, where it has been possible, a mix of rural and urban institutions. Some institutions participating in the cluster are long-time partners of the research campus, and others are new to such cooperation. While experience has demonstrated that the most effective partnerships are between institutions located near each other, recent innovations in distance learning have made productive partnerships possible over wide geographical areas. The University of Nebraska in Lincoln, for example, has established electronic relationships with Grambling State University, an historically black university in Louisiana, and Chadron State College in a rural part of Nebraska to introduce their students to more diverse institutions. Similarly, Howard University has established partnerships with Syracuse University and the University of New Hampshire.

A range of institutional types within the cluster provides not only diverse but *exemplary* experiences of institutional missions, governance structures, and faculty work. Doctoral students might, at a liberal arts college for example, attend not only department meetings but also experience a meeting of an entire faculty. At a large comprehensive university, they might learn more about how faculty members are working to integrate new technologies or how they participate in curricular change committees, that work through complex systems of department and decanal review. At a community college, they might observe as faculty members work with nontraditional students, sometimes in programs integrating academic and work experience. PFF has been particularly advantaged when doctoral students have been able to experience the *special* strengths of a variety of academic cultures.

Institutional partnerships have been established in one of three alternative ways. The most common way is for the graduate dean or other central administrator at a doctoral granting university to contact administrators at other institutions and hold a conversation about working together. That administrator may then contact department chairs or other faculty leaders about the prospects of launching this new venture. This approach relies on formal, organizational leaders and reaches out to involve departments and faculty. When Howard University and The Catholic University of America decided to work together, it marked the first time in the memory of senior administrators that the two ever collaborated—even though they are located on opposite sides of a small lake. The benefits of collaboration reached beyond the PFF program itself.

Another approach is for a doctoral department and the graduate dean to agree to proceed and then ask the faculty members in the department to contact counterparts in departments of other institutions. In any given region, a department of English, for example, will have educated many professors of English working in other kinds of institutions, and many doctoral faculty maintain informal relationships with their colleagues elsewhere. The University of Washington used this decentralized approach, where faculty leaders in the Departments of English, mathematics, sociology, and zoology created clusters based on their relationships with faculty in other institutions.

A third approach is for academic leaders at a liberal arts college or public university to approach the doctoral university in its region and explore the possibility of establishing such a program. They see themselves as prime sites to socialize neophytes to the academic profession. Indeed, some institutions have acted on their own, as have Carroll College, University of North Carolina at Asheville, and Portland State University, to create their own faculty preparation programs. They defined new types of temporary positions (one to three years) that orient new faculty to the realities of the academic life; they promote themselves as being centers of excellence in teaching, and therefore appropriate sites for training future professors.

The Steering Committee. It is necessary to find some glue that holds a cluster together and permits it to function as intended. We have learned that it is important to involve *all* the relevant constituencies from *all* participating institutions in the process of defining program goals, planning program activities, and developing long-range plans. For that reason we recommend forming a steering committee that includes representatives from each of the constituencies—graduate deans, graduate department faculty members, doctoral students, and academic administrators and faculty members in the partner institutions.

The committee usually needs to take some time to get to know each other's perspectives on preparing future faculty, understand each others' academic cultures, and get a sense of the potential contributions and pressures facing each institution. Early in the process, they might agree on the goals and the benefits they want to accrue from the relationship. Discussion might include faculty responsibilities at the different institutions, a consideration of what individuals think is strong or weak in doctoral study, exploring what they might do to improve traditional programs, and estimating the costs involved. Although they can learn a good deal about what other clusters include in their programs, they will want to design the program to take advantage of their own particular strengths and the interests and capacities of their people.

Once the program has begun operation, we have found it valuable for the steering committee to shift its focus from planning a start-up program to providing policy oversight on an ongoing basis. This ensures that all constituencies continue to have a role in the governance of the program. The steering committee can set policies, provide overall guidance to program leaders, consider specific problems that arise, make mid-course adjustments, and generally aid continuing communication among program leaders.

Responsibility for managing the cluster program is usually assigned to an individual in the doctoral university. At some places, it is an associate dean in the graduate school, and at other places it is the director of the center for teaching and learning. In some cases where the focus is in specific departments, a faculty member with particular interest in PFF programs manages it. In any event, it is essential that this manager have excellent people skills and a talent for networking among the many constituencies involved in PFF programs.

Relationships at any PFF cluster are multiple and complex, and they impose demands on already busy people. Several clusters, such as Arizona State University, have created a position of student coordinator to manage the day-to-day relationships among individuals of a cluster. Coordinators organize meetings, help students to find mentors and define meaningful learning experiences at other institutions, intercede when problems appear, identify refinements that may need to be made in the program, share information about publications, web sites, or conferences, and generally help the programs operate smoothly.

Activities of the Cluster. Several kinds of cluster activities have proved valuable, but among the most crucial are doctoral students' visits to the campus, where partner faculty on their home ground speak as experts on the roles and responsibilities of educators in that particular campus culture. A useful way to start is the *introductory visit* to a partner institution, in which a university may arrange for PFF students to visit as a group. Typically, these visits include a welcoming talk by a senior academic administrator discussing the mission and distinctive features of the institution; a discussion of roles, responsibilities, and rewards of faculty; a tour of the campus and visits to departments of special interest to the doctoral students; and ample opportunities for informal conversation with faculty members.

In addition to providing a sense of the campus, these visits help lay the groundwork for individual mentoring relationships. For participants in PFF, they also serve to clarify the roles they are expected to play, the resources available to them, and the mechanisms for making known to program leaders their concerns and recommendations. Even when the program literature (memos, brochures, etc.) includes this information, it has proven useful to revisit these themes. Although students can, and should, learn a good deal about professional issues through reading and course work, direct experience with individuals on different campuses makes this understanding both more nuanced and more profound. For those serious about PFF programming, these campus visits are just the beginning.

For most students, the core of the PFF experience consists of *individually tailored*, more intensive and repeated visits to the partner campus, where they typically engage in a variety of activities and learn about faculty life as a "junior colleague." Arrangements typically are made for selected students to attend specific future events or meetings, teach a unit of a course, establish mentoring relationships with individual faculty members, or participate in a faculty development activity. Through these guided experiences at several different campus cultures, students have come to appreciate more fully the variety of faculty roles. PFF fellows have eagerly spent as much time on the partner campuses as possible. The activities involved represent a crucial dimension of professional development for the doctoral students, helping them to understand more about such areas as tenure, governance, balancing teaching, research, and service responsibilities, new technologies, the relevance of community service, the diversity of student populations, and so on.

In addition to formally arranged individual and group visits, PFF sites have developed many ways of sustaining relationships among the participating campuses. Coordinators at the partner campuses have invited PFF students to lectures, programs, and other faculty development activities their institutions sponsor. Doctoral universities have included partner faculty on mailing lists announcing events, such as lectures and faculty development workshops and have helped to arrange for graduate faculty to establish direct connections with the partner faculty mentoring their students. Finally, many clusters have created e-mail discussion groups for participants to share information, discuss important issues, reflect critically on their experiences and the program, and provide suggestions for new initiatives.

To date most clusters have been organized and sustained on the basis of personal relations among individuals. As valuable as these dynamics have been, we believe that additional steps are required in order to create the stable interinstitutional partnerships that transcend individuals. Partnerships found in teacher education programs that contract with public and private elementary and secondary schools to provide sites for student teaching, or partnerships in medical education that create affiliation agreements with hospitals to provide sites where medical students obtain clinical experience serve as examples. We have come to believe that a formal "memorandum of agreement" can define

Duke Graduate Student Fair at Guilford College

Duke University conducts a Graduate Student Fair at Guilford College for those students interested in graduate school. Two associate deans in the graduate school take a number of PFF students from different departments to Guilford where they meet with a group of interested undergraduates and faculty. At the outset, the two deans talk about the nature and value of graduate school, describe the application and admissions processes, and offer advice. The doctoral students are invited to offer their perspectives, and the forum then turns to questions and answers. After this session are meetings in small groups, by disciplines or divisions, for more conversation that continues through a meal. Both institutions have found this a mutually beneficial activity.

the relationships between institutions in a cluster and provide a more stable framework within which the multiple relationships involved in PFF may flourish. Such a memorandum of agreement ought to include such things as the kinds of experiences that are to be provided to students, what the university and the partner want to get out of the relationship, and statements about the mutual obligations.

The complications of creating new kinds of working relationships among largely separate institutions would not be worth the effort were it not for the educational benefits that result. More than four out of five PPF students report gaining a better understanding of faculty roles and of diverse institutions and more than three of five report increased interest in an academic career, ability to compete in the job market, and knowledge about the job search process. These benefits could not be achieved without their direct involvement as junior faculty colleagues in different institutions.

This idea was well expressed by a student in English at Northwestern University in a survey:

> I have discovered that there are different pleasures and compromises associated with each academic institution. The key is knowing what the pleasures are and what compromises will be required to participate successfully in the culture of a particular college or university.

Ricki Shine (1995, p. 41), also at Northwestern in history, described her experience teaching a course at Oakton Community College and working with an assigned mentor and participating in a monthly colloquium with faculty at various partner institutions.

> I found what I had sought for so long: a community of scholars who support my teaching ambitions. I now have colleagues—graduate students and faculty members—from a variety of disciplines, and from a variety of institutions, with whom I can freely discuss pedagogical issues.

Jon Westby, a Minneapolis Community College professor who has mentored PFF students from the University of Minnesota, offered these observations, identifying a key problem and suggesting how PFF offers an important solution:

> A major theme that many graduate students have raised is the idea that their graduate advisors would not encourage them to take a position at a nonresearch institution. It's almost as if the advisor would think "it's too bad you couldn't get a real job!" Education seems to be the profession where elitism is most pronounced. Doctors and lawyers appear to be more collegial than do faculty members from different types of institutions. If I am a neurosurgeon at Johns Hopkins and you are a G.P. in a small rural town, we're still both doctors but with different specialties. But if I'm at a research university I'm an historian, and because you're at a comprehensive college or univer-

sity, you're only a history teacher. If we consider that PFF is a radical experiment in dispersing the ownership of the preparation of future faculty across a wider collaborative network, we should stress that PFF also represents a new way of thinking about the professoriate as a community of scholar/teachers embracing the full range of academic cultures.

The complex connections between the doctoral institution and the partner campuses work best against the backdrop of a spirit of collaboration. Such a spirit is not always apparent, sometimes not even present, and needs to be cultivated and re-created on an ongoing basis to keep the forces of competition and hierarchy at bay.

Macalester College Faculty Development Fund Supports PFF Activities

Macalester, like many other colleges, has a fund to support the professional development of its faculty members. When it became a partner with the University of Minnesota in the PFF program, it identified several faculty members who were interested in serving as mentors for graduate students. Eventually, faculty members were incurring costs, such as travel to professional meetings with a student, working over lunch, or purchasing instructional materials. It was determined that because the faculty members were deriving professional development benefits from their work with graduate students, these expenses could be reimbursed from the faculty development fund.

New Forms of Mentoring

Doctoral students who aspire to the professoriate need new kinds of mentors. Although they typically learn to conduct dissertation research under the direct supervision of an accomplished researcher, they seldom receive the benefit of similar support and supervision to learn about the complex of professional activities called "teaching"and "service." Deborah Stewart (1994, p. 1), the graduate dean at North Carolina State, put it: "While, if asked, many graduate students confirm that they would like more technical support for their teaching (reviewing videos of their own teaching, etc.), what they indicate they really need is a relationship, rather than a set of courses." They want to relate with an experienced faculty member so that they can discuss a range of issues and consider solutions to problems as they arise.

Graduate students may already have multiple advisors during their doctoral studies. All have a research advisor; many have a separate dissertation director. Some consider their department chair as a mentor; some others, their department's director of graduate studies. Other professors may serve, formally or informally, in a mentoring capacity. Yet, all of these have focused almost exclusively on developing expertise in the conduct of research.

The range of advisors available to doctoral students is limited, and the relationships are sometimes more hierarchical than collegial. Students often perceive advisors as controlling their academic future and, as a result, are reluctant to question their opinions on how to prepare for an academic career. Students sense they are subject to constant evaluation and believe (rightly or not) that certain topics, such as discussions about teaching and service are not welcome. Further, many students who want a college teaching career in, for example, a liberal arts college, feel they cannot reveal such aspirations to their faculty advisors, who they believe (again, rightly or not), would prefer that they seek positions in research universities.

One of the innovations of PFF is the conception of an additional kind of advisor: a faculty mentor in the same or a closely related field but *in a different institution*. The PFF mentoring experience involves close person-to-person contact with a faculty member in a partner institution and often covers the full range of faculty roles. It is more collegial and more reciprocal than the student's other advising relationships, allowing for more informal dialogue between the faculty member and the student. Because it allows students' engagement in different institutions—often ones they have never had direct contact with—they can learn more about faculty life at various institutions. The PFF mentoring relationship can and often does include research coupled with teaching and service; in fact, joint research projects are sometimes generated by these relationships.

Because these new mentoring relationships are subject to quite different interpretations, the University of Minnesota has devised a brief characterization of effective mentoring based on a synopsis of the scholarly literature. Although individuals are encouraged to exploit their own special qualities in their interactions, this synopsis provides general guidelines for a productive mentoring relationship.

It is curious that even though faculty are expected to serve as a mentors for their students, few have ever received training for that role. Since these PFF mentoring relationships are new and may not be fully understood, clusters have developed materials to guide those involved. For example, Howard University created a contract that spells out in general terms the expectations of the student and faculty member that both must sign.

Guidelines for Mentoring, University of Minnesota

WHAT A MENTOR IS

- one who empowers, encourages and supports his/her mentees
- one who is an advocate for the mentee in the department, at professional meetings, etc.
- one who encourages and values good teaching
- one who expects mentees to have their own ideas and needs
- one who can provide information about what an academic career in this field involves
- one who can help point the mentee in an appropriate direction to find resources for better teaching, for finding employment, for professional development, etc.
- one who is reasonably available
- one who involves the mentee in professional dialogue
- one who actively listens
- one who expresses positive expectations
- one who shares his/her own experiences when relevant and without removing the focus from the mentee
- one who is a positive role-model for the mentee
- one who encourages the mentee to reflect on his/her own experiences
- one who takes time to think carefully about the mentee's needs and goals
- one who can be trusted

WHAT A MENTOR IS NOT

- one who must know everything about teaching to be helpful
- one who must guide the mentee in all aspects of the mentee's professional and personal development
- one who is shaming, manipulative, arrogant, controlling, or domineering
- a parent
- one who is responsible for all aspects of the mentee's success or failure
- one who takes sole responsibility for defining the mentoring relationship

Developed by Susan Lewis (1993) with information drawn from the following sources:
- Hulling-Austin, L.L. 1990. Squishy business. In *Mentoring: Developing successful new teachers.* T.M. Bey and C.T. Holmes eds. Reston, VA: Association of Teacher Educators, 39–50. ◆ Sandler, B.R. 1993. Women as mentors: Myths and commandments. *Chronicle of Higher Education,* March 10. ◆ Coalition for Women Graduate Students. 1993. Improving the climate for women graduate students through quality mentoring at the University of Minnesota. ◆ Kay, R.S. 1990. A definition for developing self-reliance. In *Mentoring: Developing successful new teachers.* T.M. Bey and C.T. Holmes eds. Reston, VA: Association of Teacher Educators, 25–37.

The University of Minnesota holds a required mentoring workshop for faculty mentors and PFF students. Over six years this workshop for pairs of mentors and mentees has evolved from an orientation/information format to one emphasizing experiential learning. The pairs begin by sharing their individual views of collegiality and report to the larger group, then do a brief writing exercise and discussion of their desires for change or improvement. This is followed by a set of recommended strategies for the two classroom observations that the mentor is expected to do with the mentee. After a break, mentors meet as a group to discuss mentoring strategies, and mentees meet as a group to share concerns and discuss ways of becoming proactive with their mentors. The workshop concludes with a classroom observation scenario. Together they experience the vulnerabilities and difficulties of being observed or giving constructive criticism. Although brief, this introduction helps pave the way for an educational practicum.

Syracuse University has developed a seminar program to train faculty members as Teaching Mentors. The three day summer retreat and two shorter workshops in each of the following semesters address four specific objectives (Future Professoriate Project 1993, p. 3):

◆ Establish an interdisciplinary forum for the development of ideas to better prepare the future generation of the professoriate

◆ Encourage faculty in related disciplines to work together to explore common approaches to the preparation of graduate students for teaching

◆ Provide faculty with specific strategies and methodologies to establish more effective teaching assistant and teaching associate training within the context of their own disciplines

◆ Establish a heightened presence of faculty in each department to whom graduate students can turn for guidance about teaching issues.

Whatever the particular content of the mentoring experience, the dynamic of successful mentoring programs seems to run like this: At the outset the senior person is seen as the source of knowledge and wisdom that is to be passed on to the junior person; as individuals get to know each other, they discover that each possesses important knowledge and perspectives and that each can learn from the other.

Relationships that begin as hierarchical and based on one-way communication soon turn into more egalitarian relationships, and communication becomes two-way. In most cases, both parties report learning a great deal.

Graduate students in PFF have made clear that they value the opportunity to discuss their professional development with faculty *beyond* their "official"

> **"T**hanks to the PFF program, I have a deeper appreciation of how my role models' academic careers were born, and more importantly, how they were able to find, sustain, and enrich their place in the profession."
>
> 1996–1997 PFF Fellow, mathematics, Northwestern University

research advisor. The mentor program helps to legitimate discussions that are felt to be taboo in their own department, it gives students access to new and different kinds of faculty expertise, and it also gives them a growing network of professional colleagues who are often helpful in the job search.

Understanding the Centrality of the Faculty

Preparation of doctoral students is rooted in academic departments. Departments are characterized by distinctive cultures, involving their own values, practices, procedures, and guidelines. Thus, new forms of partnerships and new kinds of mentoring require leadership from faculty members in both the doctoral university and its partners. And since these innovations are by definition nontraditional, faculty participants—at least initially—are those who are able and willing to think "outside the box" and experiment with new ways of educating doctoral students about the realities of faculty life. In the long run, these innovations will not survive unless they are rooted in the lives of the academic departments. Issues can best be discussed separately for the different kinds of institutions.

At the Doctoral University. We have learned that the ways PFF programs are initiated in universities helps to influence faculty and departmental ownership. In the first phase of the PFF program, we awarded grants to graduate schools on the condition that they follow the guidelines that were developed, including taking steps to secure faculty leadership and departmental ownership for them. However, this arrangement inadvertently placed faculty members and academic departments in a secondary, or derivative, position. Graduate deans were placed in the position of eliciting interest of faculty members, which all were able to do. But the dynamic was for the faculty members to feel that they were being asked to do something that their dean wanted them to do. It was less their idea than the dean's, and in most departments it faced opposition from some who were unaware of the benefits of PFF and saw PFF as a threat to their traditional emphasis on research. Although this strategy—

the dean's encouragement—generated strong faculty leadership, only a few individuals were involved, and most departments gave only partial support.

In this context, some universities adopted centralized strategies to operate their PFF programs. They were often connected to already centralized faculty and TA development programs, as a way to operate with modest faculty support. This method has worked well, because it required only a few faculty members to become involved as instructors, sometimes even on a limited basis, in teaching PFF courses. It even allowed rapid expansion of their programs, because it did not rely on many departments committing to devise and run the program. Yet, it did little to bring more faculty into the program or to secure departmental ownership.

The Universities of Cincinnati, Kentucky, and Wisconsin at Milwaukee have since created core PFF courses offered by the graduate school and have coordinated the relationships with cluster partners. This strategy left the staff of the graduate school or faculty development program running PFF and constantly trying to secure the support of faculty members and departments. Following this strategy, the University of Minnesota has secured the approval of seventy-five of its 110 doctoral programs for their students to participate in the PFF program. The departmental approval strategy constitutes permission for students to participate; it does not constitute a commitment to make the program succeed.

From the start, some universities, such as Florida State, Indiana, and Washington, took a different tack, by emphasizing the importance of departmental ownership; graduate deans initially elicited from departments willingness to participate. Departments designed their own programs around the interests of their faculty, and faculty leaders contacted their colleagues in departments in partner institutions. This much more decentralized strategy placed the responsibility for PFF program development and operation in the hands of departments, and it seems to have created more departmental commitment to PFF concepts and programs. Even so, the number of faculty knowledgeable and committed to PFF continued to be small. At the same time, leaders of these departmentally based programs found it necessary to establish university-wide activities, such as courses on generic issues of teaching or professional practice, gatherings of students to discuss issues across departments, guidelines to assure quality in very different programs, and assessment.

Both types of programs continue to search for a balance between centralized and decentralized activities, between departmental and graduate school elements.

During Phase II, some universities used a different strategy. The University of Nebraska, for example, took an extreme departmental approach. The PFF program director, a professor in the department of communication studies, talked with department chairs *as a faculty colleague*. After learning about the ideas and experiences in PFF programs, the chairs took the idea to other leaders of the departments and secured their support. In this context, the faculty and departments "own" the programs in ways that are rare elsewhere. In addition, the steering committee of the Nebraska cluster includes faculty leaders of these departments.

Regardless of the way the program is established, PFF leaders have found it wise to connect with other faculty structures and activities to give it a supportive infrastructure and legitimize it in the face of some faculty skepticism. Duke, Kentucky, and New Hampshire, for instance, connect their PFF programs with centers for teaching and learning. The faculty development activities are a natural complement for PFF activities, with PFF students and faculty members often participating together in a seminar or workshop. Several universities connect PFF to graduate teaching assistant development programs, whether these are departmental or university-wide. Those engaged in such development work have generally been supportive of the enriched, forward-looking, and more complex conception of professional development that PFF brings to their work. As a result, these staffs typically contribute a great deal to program planning and operation.

Despite all our efforts, faculty and departmental ownership continues to be a problem, and we continue to chip away at it with presentations at meetings of learned societies, reflections from PFF participants, assessments of programs, and spreading information through publications and electronic means.

In our most ambitious undertaking to date, we have embarked on the third phase of PFF: a collaboration, with support from the National Science Foundation, to help reshape doctoral preparation of future faculty in the sciences and mathematics. The design calls for grants to be awarded to professional societies in biology, chemistry, physics, mathematics, and computing. Each society has a) initiated a national conversation about better ways to prepare future faculty, b) conducted a national competition and awarded funds to at least four departments, c) assessed and monitored progress, and d) highlighted promising practices in its meetings and publications. A similar proposal has been approved to work with six learned societies in the humanities and social sciences to develop model PFF programs in communications, English, history, political science, psychology, and sociology.

The goal is to combine this strategy of speaking to faculty members through their disciplines with the original strategy of working through university graduate schools. We expect that this new initiative will reach faculty members in more powerful ways than our original approach and help them see the significance of PFF for preparing their future colleagues in their own fields. Indeed, the National Communication Association already developed its own Preparing

Future Communication Faculty Program, awarding seed grants to four graduate departments to develop model programs. Several leaders of that association were leaders in graduate schools in the PFF program, who saw the potential PFF offered for their fields. Our new approach to create faculty and departmental ownership for PFF programs will build directly on that effort.

At Partner Institutions. Since the prototypical PFF experience is direct person-to-person contact between a student and a faculty member at a partner institution, the active, committed involvement of partner faculty is essential. Their role in these programs is genuinely unprecedented, since it does not fall within their ordinary duties as faculty members at their institutions and requires additional work. But despite some initial hesitation concerning the biases of the culture of graduate education that looks down on their institutions and the time that might be involved, they have developed deep commitments to the students they mentor and have worked hard to help them understand the mysteries of the academic profession.

PFF programs are established in partner institutions in basically three distinct ways. The most common way is for the graduate dean at the doctoral university to contact the chief academic officer at a potential partner institution to raise the possibility of developing a new partnership. Assuming that there is interest among the administrators, then the provost or academic dean works with the graduate dean to identify possible participant departments in both institutions to participate. S/He then typically contacts the department chair or other influential faculty member in the department about the possibility of cooperating in the program.

In some cases, the program is initiated by partner institutions. Administrators in these institutions sometimes hear about the PFF program and sense the benefit for their schools and faculty, but since they need the involvement of a doctoral university in their region, they initiate the conversation. In other cases, the connections are between the faculty members of the departments directly. Frequently, the flagship university has provided the doctoral education for many faculty members of departments in various colleges and universities in the region, and long term professional relationships exist among several faculty. Department leaders utilize these professional networks to invite involvement in the PFF initiative. Although this is an effective means to generate department and faculty ownership of the program, it is our experience that these department initiatives are stronger if they can be connected, usually through the graduate school, with similar initiatives in other departments. The universities in the PFF program that have started by developing department approaches, such as the University of Washington, have found it useful to buttress those efforts with central activities, so that students and faculty members can exchange ideas and experiences with colleagues in other departments. Similarly, some universities that began with central activities, such as Arizona State University, have found it important to develop more activities in the departments. Department activities can be buttressed with central activities, whether at the graduate school or some professional development unit. Also, by involving the graduate school, departments have been able to gain access to additional resources.

However the programs are established, the partner faculty are essential to the success of PFF. Their ongoing participation has been sustained by a variety of means that assure meaningful involvement and recognition for their contributions. This has included:

◆ a commitment to giving partner faculty "co-ownership" of PFF, consulting with them as plans for subsequent semesters and years develop and assuring that partner faculty are represented on the steering committee and at national PFF meetings

◆ professional recognition for their work: e.g., honoraria, professional development support, and release time when possible, but also including their names and contributions on program literature

◆ opportunities otherwise unavailable at the graduate university (e.g., special library privileges, Internet and World Wide Web access)

◆ invitations to lectures, convocations, or special events in the university or department

◆ the encouragement of collaborative research activities with graduate students and graduate faculty

◆ an invitation to join PFF graduates and their research advisor for an annual culminating event.

Faculty Views. Through surveys of nearly 192 partner faculty, as well as eighty-three graduate faculty, and other, more direct communications from them, we have learned much about their involvement in PFF. From the very beginning nearly all partner faculty were committed to the fundamental purposes of the program. They thought this more thorough preparation was "the right thing to do," and many appreciated the opportunity, otherwise unavailable to them, to work closely with advanced doctoral students. Fundamentally, partner faculty *enjoy* the mentoring role, convinced that they are making a difference in the professional growth of a younger colleague. As one said, "I view it as a generative activity—passing information, ideas, expertise to the next generation of scholar-teachers."

Faculty members at partner institutions report participation in PFF is a valuable source of their professional growth. The majority of faculty involved in PFF are senior professors at both the universities and partner institutions. That means that PFF can be a vehicle for the renewal of senior faculty as they work for the education of their junior colleagues. In fact, PFF is a powerful stimulus for the professional development of all those who are involved.

What are some of the benefits reported by faculty members? Partner faculty report the following benefits:

◆ gaining knowledge about current research through contact with graduate students

◆ being stimulated to reflect on their roles as a faculty member

◆ getting to know faculty colleagues from other institutions in the cluster

◆ renewing relationships with faculty at the doctoral university

◆ broadening perspectives on their work by seeing it through the eyes of junior colleagues

◆ seeing new ways to teach an old course

◆ looking at trends and issues affecting the future of the profession

◆ increasing enthusiasm in their own teaching

Virtually all 285 faculty members from all institutions surveyed in 1995 and 1996 said they would recommend their PFF program to others. Among the 141 surveyed in 1996, only two said they would not recommend it. The two reasons cited were the distance between the two campuses consumed too much time in travel, and a particular graduate student was said to lack commitment to follow through. It is significant that among the faculty actually involved in PFF programs, they are nearly unanimous in their support.

> Fundamentally, partner faculty enjoy the mentoring role, convinced that they are making a difference in the professional growth of a younger colleague.

Faculty members at *both* types of institutions are concerned about time and money. Most faculty members worked in PFF not as part of their formal workload but as an overload. This is not unusual for innovative programs, but the long-term success of PFF requires it factored into workload. Also, the graduate faculty pointed out the lack of incentives regarding their work in PFF programs—but one more aspect of problematic reward structures. Many partner faculty who are involved receive modest professional development funds as compensation. Depending on the amount of work involved, faculty who mentor a student often receive $300–$500 which they can use to purchase books or software or travel to a professional meeting. Perhaps not surprisingly, faculty report valuing not so much the amount of the compensation but the fact that one's contribution is recognized and appreciated.

Faculty participants—graduate and partner faculty alike—report that over time the stereotypes of colleagues at other types of institutions collapse, and they acquire an enhanced appreciation of mutual concerns and interests and a richer understanding of the academy in all its diversity. PFF appears to be a useful vehicle to enrich the awareness of professional issues of faculty members at both research universities and their partner institutions through their joint involvement in welcoming the next generation of college professors into the academy. The words of a former graduate dean at The Ohio State University put it well:

> The energy and commitment that graduate students and partner faculty have brought to the discussions have enabled research faculty to affirm and support teaching in a way that is usually not possible, given the culture of the surroundings.

CHAPTER 3

Student Experiences

Doctoral students are enthusiastic about what they learn in the new faculty preparation programs. The quality of their education and the effective preparation for their careers in the academy are, after all, the basic reasons for establishing PFF programs. If students gain the benefits claimed by advocates of these programs, then the complex efforts to devise new institutional partnerships, develop new forms of mentoring, and engage faculty members and departments in new behaviors are justified. Indeed, we believe that the valuable learning experiences among students in these programs suggest a successful strategy to engage faculty members and departments: listen to the experiences of students in these new faculty preparation programs and learn how these programs enrich the students' education and improve their chances for a successful academic career. We have found that the students are the best advocates for PFF programs. Although graduate faculty originally may be skeptical of an activity that takes time away from research, they typically are willing to support such programs if deemed in the best interest of their students and if the students want them. One graduate faculty member spoke for many when he said about his student's involvement in a PFF program, "If she wants it, I'll support it."

Evidence about the experiences of students and the learning they derive from PFF programs comes from several sources: reflective analyses by graduate students as a part of their PFF programs, papers by students delivered at a variety of professional conferences, anecdotes, and testimonies contained in brochures and on web sites. The most systematic information is contained in two program-wide surveys of students. Increasingly, we are hearing reports from students who have obtained academic jobs, and assessments from universities about how well their PFF programs prepared alumni for their responsibilities. The preponderance of early evidence leads to the conclusion that the faculty preparation programs are superior to traditional doctoral study in preparing future college professors.

An Emergent Pattern of Disproportionate Success

A pattern seems to be emerging in which PFF students are disproportionately selected for competitive awards. At the national level, the American Association for Higher Education announced a new award providing full support for graduate students to attend its national meeting in 1999. Seven individuals were selected from among fifty nominations, and four were from PFF programs at the universities of Colorado, Minnesota, and Nebraska, and Arizona State. Selection criteria included potential for leadership in teaching and learning, strong sense of civic responsibility, and commitment to contribute to the development of others as leaders, scholars, and citizens. Similarly, at the cluster level, the Faculty Women's Association at Arizona State gives an award for scholarship, research, and leadership. Since 1995, four of the eight awards have gone to PFF students. Although the numbers are small, these competitions conducted by organizations independently of PFF programs are another indication that PFF gives students an edge over their peers who have not been involved.

Voices of Graduate Students

Students have had many opportunities to comment on their experiences in the PFF program. As with any new experience, individuals do not fully comprehend what it means at the outset and only slowly come to appreciate what PFF means and its ramifications for them.

The orientation of new PFF students at Arizona State includes short descriptions by second-year students of their experiences during the first year. Cristal McGill, an educational psychology student, described her earliest PFF experiences this way:

Upon returning to campus from my summer commitments, I was congratulated by some of the department professors and staff for being accepted into the Preparing Future Faculty program. I did not think much about those salutations until our first PFF meeting. During that meeting, Dean Bianca Bernstein spoke at the initial PFF orientation in reference to the honor of being accepted to the PFF program. I began to realize this was a bigger opportunity than I had initially anticipated.

She continued:

The PFF program opened my thoughts to new ideas for cross discipline work with different perspectives and new insights. Personally the PFF program helped me build confidence in myself as a scholar, as well as what I have to bring to the table as a young professor.

> **P**ersonally the PFF program helped me build confidence in myself as a scholar, as well as what I have to bring to the table as a young professor.

The value of the experience often does not become apparent until participants interact with others. The following two comments are from students who had participated in PFF for several months and then attended conferences. They shared their insights on the PFF listserv.

I went to a conference and what struck me profoundly . . . was how much more savvy I was than the other graduate students there. Not only was I aware of this difference, but other people commented on it. It was only in a professional situation like a conference that I could measure the extent to which PFF has achieved its aim of professionalizing and preparing us for the professoriate.

I echo the sentiments of . . . cohorts who have attended conferences and felt 'one step ahead' of the rest of the graduate student world. I met so many people using PFF as a 'springboard' for conversations—deans and department chairs were truly interested in the project.

Reflections by students at the end of their programs offer additional perspectives. An English student, in an essay reflecting on his experience at the University of Cincinnati, wrote:

My experience with the PFF project has been one of the highlights — if not *the* (italics in original) highlight of my doctoral study at the University of Cincinnati. To be honest, I was a little uncertain of how the experience would pan out, considering my status as an advanced doctoral candidate finishing my dissertation. I expected that I would be hearing a number of things I had already heard while at UC. What I soon learned, however, was that UC's mission was not the mission of many other colleges and universities. In the end, I believe that it was my participation in the PFF project that was the key factor in my being offered a tenure track assistant professor position [at a comprehensive university].

An exercise science student at Arizona State University, writing on her "capstone experience," said PFF "has been, without question, *one of the most meaningful parts of my graduate school experience* (italics added)." In her conclusion, she wrote,

> The first test of the value of PFF was my successful job search. I am convinced that our seminars, the participation phase experiences, interaction with fellows from other disciplines, and interaction with faculty from all types of institutions, has helped prepare me for life in academia.

A student in French at a pilot PFF program at The Ohio State University said that as a panelist at a state-wide conference, "I don't feel like a student. I feel like a professional pursuing a career."

As these comments indicate, a surprising number of students say that PFF is *the best or one of the best parts* of their doctoral study. While this is a high compliment of the program, it can be seen as a stinging criticism of traditional doctoral studies. One wonders if students' active involvement in PFF activities, their being treated as junior colleagues, their sense of being a part of a real and meaningful process of education was somehow missing in the rest of their doctoral studies. If so, why is that the case, and what can be done to capture the vitality that pervades faculty preparation programs? Treating students with greater respect and sharing professionally meaningful perspectives is easy and inexpensive.

In addition to these statements, we might look at comments from students at a single university. The following comments, and more, may be found on the PFF World Wide Web site at Northwestern University (http://nuinfo.nwu.edu/graduate/PFF/).

> It was great being mentored—you get so much out of the program when you are closely involved with someone at another institution. You learn about the school, what it's like to teach there, and you get to know the faculty. (HISTORY STUDENT)

> I have heard insights from faculty at other institutions, who are perhaps more likely to have experimented with alternative teaching techniques, such as the use of computers in the classroom or calculus reform projects. (MATH STUDENT)

I feel that I am gaining twenty steps on some of my departmental colleagues who are not benefitting from this program. (HISTORY STUDENT)

PFF has provided a foundational and life-changing experience. The program supplied a provocative forum for intellectual growth and critical reflection on our system of higher education and graduate training along with crucial discussions of balancing and integrating teaching, research, and service. (CHEMISTRY STUDENT)

PFF has convinced me of the need to formulate some professional goals before I suddenly find myself interviewing for a job. (PHYSICS STUDENT)

The abundance of these stories convinces leaders of PFF programs that students in these programs tend to be more advanced than their counterparts who have not participated in them. In fact, several concluded that these students are one to two years more mature and sophisticated professionally than their nonparticipating peers.

Survey of Graduate Students

We conducted program-wide surveys of doctoral students in PFF programs during the Spring of 1995 and again in 1996. A total of 357 usable questionnaires were returned, making a large but not necessarily random sample of PFF participants. In fact, the questionnaires were prepared centrally with instructions that cluster leaders were to distribute them to those individuals "most involved" in PFF programs, leaving the definition of that term to each of the cluster coordinators. We were interested in learning about the views of those persons who were full participants in these programs, not of individuals who may have attended an isolated event or two.

Since complete report of the results of the surveys can be found elsewhere (Pruitt-Logan, Gaff, and Weibl 1998; Gaff and Pruitt-Logan 1998), we will only mention a few of the highlights here. The students who completed questionnaires were demographically similar in both years. In 1996 the students were distributed across academic disciplines: twenty-nine in English, twenty-three in other humanities fields, thirty-seven in natural sciences, forty-four in social sciences, sixteen in mathematics, and twenty-two in education and other professional fields. Slightly more than half were women, and 90 percent said they were within two years of finishing their degrees. In both years, more than three quarters were white and the rest were ethnic minorities, of which African Americans were the largest group.

When asked why they decided to participate in PFF, students most often said they wanted to learn about faculty roles and explore their interest in becoming a professor. Most also wanted to enhance their teaching skills and learn about institutions other than research universities. We asked students to rate several benefits they might have derived from participation in PFF. More than four of five said PFF helped them to understand faculty roles, and helped increase their awareness of diverse institutions. More than three of five indicated their participation strengthened their interest in an academic career, enhanced their ability to compete in the job market, and assisted them in understanding the job search process.

In both surveys, when asked whether they would recommend PFF to other doctoral students, 99 percent of the students said "yes." Seventy-three percent said they would recommend their PFF program without reservation because of the insights it provided.

One consequence of the faculty preparation program in which students are exposed to different kinds of institutions may be that it broadens their career options. The assumption in most graduate programs, though perhaps unstated, is that students who wish to be professors should aspire to a position in a research university. In the first survey, we asked students what kinds of institutions they hoped to work for in their first job. Forty-five percent chose a liberal arts college, 21 percent a research university, 16 percent a comprehensive college or university, and four percent a community college (the remainder did not answer). In the second survey we asked students to rate various types of institutions according to how attractive they were. Seventy-one percent of the respondents found a liberal arts college "very attractive," as did 68 percent for a comprehensive institution, 52 percent for a research university, and 16 percent for a community college. It appears that PFF makes it acceptable for students to explore work in places other than research universities. Perhaps PFF programs provide a safe context for expressing this interest to their professors who are perceived to prefer their students to work in research universities.

We did additional analyses to determine if the extent of student involvement affected reported benefits. It turned out that those most involved reported greater benefits, such as greater understanding of faculty roles, awareness of diverse institutions, and ability to compete in the job market. It appears that involvement begets greater benefits—the more involvement, the greater the benefit. Of course, the reverse might be true, that is, those who are drawing the most benefits avail themselves of the opportunities offered.

The important point is that this survey confirmed the essence of the reports from individuals about the program and about the benefits they have derived.

The Job Market and Reports from Alumni

A number of PFF graduates have taken academic positions, and their perspectives constitute additional information about the effectiveness of these new programs.

Duke University participated in the forerunner to the PFF program, and Leigh DeNeef (1996), associate dean of the graduate school, reports that he tracked seventy-six students over five years. Of the approximately one-half who had graduated, virtually all found an academic position. Nine were in research universities, sixteen in liberal arts colleges, and nine in comprehensive universities, roughly comparable with the results of Duke's graduate school as a whole. He drew three major conclusions from the faculty preparation programs he directed: 1) despite fears from some faculty members, these programs do not "corrupt" students; 2) the programs "guard [students] against too narrow a set of intellectual and research interests" and "keep them competitive for the full range of academic employment;" and 3) the graduate faculty have little experience with the realities of the job market at other types of institutions. He concludes that "Successfully preparing future faculty for a complex and difficult job market is simply not something that any single institution—and certainly not any single faculty mentor—can do alone."

> **V**irtually all said they believed that involvement in the program was helpful in securing their positions.

Syracuse University, too, operated its own faculty preparation program before it was selected to become part of the national PFF program (Tice, Gaff, and Pruitt-Logan 1998). Telephone interviews with more that seventy alumni who had participated revealed that over 90 percent had secured academic employment in the type of position they were seeking. Virtually all said they believed that involvement in the program was helpful in securing their positions. That helps to explain why its Syracuse Future Professoriate Project budget has been fully supported by the university since 1995.

It was anticipated that experience in a faculty preparation program might be valued by hiring institutions. In our second survey, we asked students who had been involved in academic searches to tell us about their experiences. Fifty-two had been in a search and 79 percent of them indicated that PFF had been "very" or "moderately useful." Student comments indicated that they felt clearer about the positions for which they were applying and were better able to develop appropriate cover letters, curriculum vitae, and professional portfolios. Most said that those who were conducting the searches seemed impressed with the fact that they had been involved in a faculty preparation experience. This preliminary evidence suggests that PFF experience is helpful to candidates for academic positions.

Another perspective on the value of PFF programs comes from alumni who are currently in academic positions. Most of this information consists of anecdotes from numerous individuals. Many of these new faculty members have thoughtfully incorporated their PFF experience in a professional portfolio and reflected on its specific benefits to them. One of these is Tina Evans, currently assistant professor of political science at Bethune-Cookman College. A summary of her PFF activities at Howard University, where she was selected for the first cohort of PFF students, included workshops on preparing performance objectives, ethical issues in graduate education, instructional strategies for students with disabilities, teaching across cultural lines, successful career paths in higher education, and mentoring graduate students for faculty careers; a course titled American National Government; and a panel on "Race, IQ, and Public Policy: The Bell Curve." At partner institutions she taught an American government course at Marymount and team taught a black politics course at Bowie State, participated in a workshop on preparing for testing at Catholic University, was videotaped lecturing and making a panel presentation at Bowie State University, and attended faculty and departmental meetings.

At the 5th Annual Conference on the Education and Employment of Graduate Teaching Assistantships, Dr. Evans made a presentation on "The Professional Apprenticeship" where she summarized what she gained from her PFF experiences. She highlighted her development of a professional teaching and research portfolio and opportunities to expand her professional network. She said she had three mentors who successfully guided her through each semester and wrote letters of recommendation that she used to obtain her current position. She also says that she has been able to successfully balance responsibilities that she has to the Faculty Association at Bethune-Cookman with her teaching and research.

In sum, PFF students and alumni provide an abundance of testimony about the value of these new faculty preparation programs.

Stimulating Market Demand for More Comprehensive Preparation

These efforts have started to create a market demand for the graduates of new faculty preparation programs. Although we have further to go before the academic job market recognizes the value of PFF programs, a beginning has been made.

To assist PFF participants in competing in the job market, a brief statement of the purposes and character of the PFF program is provided for participants to include in their dossiers. In addition, we operate a clearinghouse of information about available jobs, informing deans and other members of electronic networks about the PFF program and the availability of a pool of comprehensively prepared doctoral students seeking faculty positions. The clearinghouse requests brief descriptions of job openings. This information is sent to each of the clusters for availability to the students seeking positions.

Several groups of institutions are issuing statements about the qualities they seek in new faculty. These statements stress the importance of more qualifications than research or scholarly expertise. The academic deans of the Commonwealth Partnership (undated), a group of Pennsylvania liberal arts colleges, for instance, issued an open letter to new Ph.D.s about what they expect of new faculty. They identified five qualities:

1. a serious commitment to both teaching and research, especially the kind of research that involves students

2. ability to place the discipline in a larger intellectual context and flexibility to cross disciplinary boundaries

3. strong communication skills and willingness to teach those skills as well as the content of the discipline

4. willingness to engage in a great deal of social interaction

5. commitment to teach as much by who they are as by what they say.

At these liberal arts colleges, Ph.D.s coming out of comprehensive preparation programs would seem to hold an advantage over those educated in traditional doctoral study that only stresses research.

Similarly, the Associated New American Colleges is preparing a statement about the qualities they seek in new faculty members, a statement certain to resemble the qualities PFF aspires to cultivate.

Problems of Participation

Students involved in faculty preparation programs have encountered some problems, particularly during the start-up phase of the programs. As mentioned earlier, the problems most commonly identified by our surveys are time and logistics. Time-to-degree is a very serious matter, as the length of time to complete a doctoral degree has increased. Currently the median registered time-to-degree—the time enrolled in educational programs between the baccalaureate and doctorate degrees—is about seven years, ranging from a low of 6.4 years in the natural sciences, to a high of 8.4 in the humanities (National Academy of Science 1996). Leaders in doctoral education agree that time to degree should not be increased and are seeking ways to reduce it. It is an issue that concerns us.

Faculty preparation programs can increase time to degree, especially those that involve substantial immersion experiences—usually teaching—at another campus. "Full immersion" can be valuable as a learning experience, but it is demanding in terms of time. Especially for students who have served as a teaching assistant, we have encouraged program designs in which students teach a few classes or a unit of a course and discuss with a faculty member plans for that segment with de-briefing afterward. Several visits to the partner campus, including opportunities to interact with faculty members in meetings and around significant campus issues, can provide a rich learning experience without adding significantly to the time required for a degree. This is especially true if the graduate department can integrate the PFF program into the doctoral program so as to streamline other requirements or find ways for them to be met within the PFF program.

> The majority of participants do not perceive that participation increases the time to degree.

As a rule, streamlining or reducing requirements to accommodate PFF is anathema to a department. However, Carol Simpson Stern, former graduate dean at Northwestern, has offered a useful guideline for determining whether a department ought to require a given course: Courses that are *significantly different* from the usual array of courses and those that add greater value by virtue of their distinctive new ideas and perspectives should be given priority over those that are similar to other offerings. By this criterion, PFF programs, being different from what students would otherwise study, should receive priority over, for example, a course dealing with one more author, research technique, time period, or area of the world. It appears that it is this *sense of differentness* from what they usually study that may account for the large number of students who say that their PFF experience was the *most valuable* part of their doctoral study.

In our survey of students, 83 percent reported that PFF participation had not increased their time to degree, although 14 percent reported that it did. Caution must be used in interpreting these results, since they are self-reports rather than university records, and they are offered by students before completing their degrees. Nonetheless, the majority of participants do not perceive that participation increases the time to degree. Further, some students say they do not care if it does increase the time they need to earn a degree, as long as they are learning valuable lessons that will enhance their careers.

On the other hand, a few students—four percent in the survey—indicated that PFF shortened their time to degree. Apparently, for them, the experience

A Resolution Supporting Preparing Future Faculty

The National Association of Graduate and Professional Students
Annual Meeting 1996
NAGPS General Session Bill GS-96-5

Author(s): Jessica Sheetz, Marquette University;
Granville Simmons, Howard University

WHEREAS, graduate students interested in careers in the professoriate recognize the need for improved training programs in teaching; and

WHEREAS, this need has historically not been addressed; and

WHEREAS, the PFF Initiative is established nationally in the form of seventeen models that provide a framework for teacher training at the Masters and Ph.D. levels, and builds on existing teaching assistant and teaching fellowship programs;

Be it therefore RESOLVED that NAGPS encourages its member GSOs to investigate the possibility of creating organizations that adopt the AACU-CGS "Preparing Future Faculty" philosophy and objectives relating to pedagogical skill building (e.g. learning styles, assessment and teaching philosophies) and professional development (e.g. rank and tenure, job search, and interview); and

Be it further RESOLVED that NAGPS encourages graduate students across all disciplines to take responsibility for their professional development as teachers and future faculty members by:

- Placing new emphasis on teaching as scholarship
- Exploring and developing learning styles given growing diversity within student populations (e.g. age, ethnicity, gender, race, sexual preferences)
- Examining issues of technology in the classroom
- Heightening awareness of faculty roles and responsibilities
- Completing a professional portfolio

Finally, be it RESOLVED that NAGPS urges that these activities be formally acknowledged by disciplinary departments and the degree granting institution (e.g. through course credit, certificate, or notes on transcript)

of being treated as a junior faculty colleague and becoming involved in faculty life at partner institutions introduced a greater sense of realism into their studies. It appears to help some students to become more goal oriented and to complete their studies more quickly in order to get on with their careers.

Logistics can be a problem, particularly the difficulties of connecting with faculty members at other campuses, arranging for visits around schedules of busy people, and traveling to another campus. As we pointed out in Chapter Two, the logistical complications can be minimized by selecting partners close to the university, developing mechanisms to connect individuals with each other, and using program coordinators to smooth arrangements. Nonetheless, complications do arise, such as an occasional traffic jam.

Encouragement is another problem. While the majority of students report receiving encouragement for PFF participation from their department head (92 percent), student peers (88 percent), departmental faculty (88 percent), and major advisor (82 percent), this support is not complete. Eighteen percent report they were discouraged by their major advisor, 14 percent by other department faculty, 12 percent by other doctoral students, and eight percent by the department chair. Mixed messages like these continue to be sent; to be effective, more faculty members and students need to understand and support the PFF initiative.

Obviously, not all students involved in faculty preparation programs are successful in a difficult job market; factors other than participation in a faculty preparation program are involved in whatever success they have. PFF programs are about more than getting a job. Nonetheless, the evidence is growing that faculty preparation programs equip students to become more sophisticated about faculty life in different institutions and help them secure positions, even in a tight job market. Early anecdotes also suggest that these programs might contribute to the early career success of new faculty members.

The students who have participated in PFF programs are sufficiently impressed with their significance that they led the National Association of Graduate and Professional Students to unanimously endorse their philosophy and objectives (See page 47).

In sum, evidence we gathered validates the importance of these new faculty preparation programs. Our conclusions are that traditional doctoral study prepares *good researchers*. Teaching assistant programs and the professional development programs that support student teachers prepare *good teaching assistants*. Faculty preparation programs prepare *good assistant professors*, an outcome that subsumes and goes beyond the other two. These conclusions may be why students aspiring to an academic career are so motivated to participate in these new programs and are virtually unanimous in recommending them to others.

CHAPTER 4

Meeting Future Challenges

D espite the substantial progress that has been made, formidable challenges remain. Several steps are required to sustain current PFF programs, and other changes throughout the academy also will be needed if the "culture of preparation" is to change. And PFF programs, like doctoral education and the faculty themselves, must ensure inclusiveness. Each of these sets of challenges will be discussed separately.

Sustaining Faculty Preparation Programs

1. Sustaining the clusters. Clusters involve innovative partnerships among diverse institutions that were originally formed to meet the conditions of a grant. We know that structures assembled largely to secure outside funding are vulnerable after the funding ends. Further, some clusters were assembled by a single individual, utilizing that person's friendships or professional networks, tenuous grounds for a permanent *institutional* relationship. When that person leaves or takes on other responsibilities, clusters fall apart. If they are to be sustained,

PFF programs must enjoy the strong commitment of a critical mass of participants, individuals who understand their power and can explain it to skeptical colleagues. Also, they must be rooted in an infrastructure that cannot easily be dismantled, such as institutional policies governing partnerships and collaboration among institutions. They should include provisions for memoranda of understanding, a steering committee, a cadre of mentors who expect to continue with the program, and close relationships among faculty members throughout the cluster.

What are the prospects that the clusters can be sustained? There is evidence that clusters can survive without grant funding. During the academic year 1996–1997, the year between the first two phases of the program, clusters received no funding. Yet all of the ten involved in the current phase as well as some others in Phase I continued their cluster arrangements; many expanded their programs. Also, some institutions in the clusters have expanded their relationships based on mutual interests. For example, new teaching assistant exchanges have been arranged at Marquette University and the University of Wisconsin, Milwaukee and between Howard and Catholic Universities. With no money changing hands, doctoral students at these universities can work at institutions with missions and student bodies that are different from those at their home departments.

By the time the Pew Phase II grant ends in 2000, we expect that institutional policies governing clusters will have been put in place. Also, we hope that enough individuals will have been so involved—deep enough bonds between individuals will have been forged and enough leaders of departments and institutions will have seen the very real benefits that accrue from these partnerships—that they will see to it that the program continues.

2. Integrating PFF into doctoral programs. As is common for academic innovations, most PFF programs started as an "add-on" to traditional doctoral studies. Students were encouraged to attend a series of workshops or seminars or, in some cases, to enroll in one or more courses, for example, on teaching in the field. In some cases the courses were not allowed to count toward the requirements for the degree. Faculty members were enticed to teach a class or to work as a mentor on teaching or service roles, often without compensation or release time. All of these are common practices to try out new ideas and experiment with alternative approaches. But they are not conducive to long-term success of an initiative. The institution or department must decide to embrace PFF approaches, and integrate them into the regular and routine life of the organization.

Increasingly, we are seeing the PFF experiences packaged as courses offered either by the graduate school or by departments, in some cases both. These courses bear academic credit that can be counted toward a degree, although there is considerable variation on this matter among departments. Similarly, the mentor experience is packaged as a practicum course at some places, such as the University of Minnesota. Courses are familiar ways to structure learning experiences so that they can fit comfortably into academic programs.

Recognition for completion of a course of study in PFF is another way of integrating it into traditional doctoral studies. Such recognition takes the form of a Certificate in College Teaching at Syracuse, and either a cognate or master's degree in college teaching at the University of New Hampshire. Marquette University notes the completion of a PFF experience on the student's curriculum transcript.

Awarding credit for PFF courses, giving recognition to those who complete a PFF program, and including questions on an examination are practices that signal the seriousness of this kind of program.

A stronger signal of the importance of PFF is inclusion of a question on teaching and learning on the qualifying examination. Although this practice is not very common, it is required in the School of Journalism at Indiana University, where students are prepared by taking a course on Teaching Mass Communications in College, enrolling in a practicum for doctoral students teaching one of the introductory courses, attending "shop talks" every other Friday, working with a mentor, and developing a portfolio. Although not a part of the national PFF program, the College of Communications at Pennsylvania State University also requires all Ph.D. students to answer a question on learning theory on the qualifying examination. In addition, all doctoral students in communications must take a course in pedagogy and curriculum development, serve as a teaching assistant, teach at least one course as an instructor, and develop a teaching portfolio.

Awarding credit for PFF courses, giving recognition to those who complete a PFF program, and including questions on an examination are practices that signal the seriousness of this kind of program. Moreover, they are ways to make PFF integral to departmental offerings, not add-ons.

Ideally, we would like to see an identifiable PFF track that would be available to those interested in pursuing this course of study. Just as a student in psychology, for instance, can elect to concentrate on school, organizational, or clinical specializations, and then pursue the specific requirements for that track, so could a department establish a PFF track for those students interested in exploring an academic career. It might contain one course on teaching and another on the academic profession; it could include a semester of work with a faculty mentor at another institution, direct experience with any of a number of faculty roles (serving on a committee, reviewing applications for professional development funds, participating on a task force on the future of the university, etc.), assembling a portfolio that includes a reflective and integrative essay, and questions on a portion of the qualifying examination. Students electing to take this track would be able to know that it is a legitimate part of doctoral study with proper organizational support, not an additional burden.

3. Extending PFF programs throughout institutions. This issue can be viewed in several ways, for example, numbers. At first blush, PFF participants appear to be only a small fraction of the entire graduate student population at any university. In fact, the majority of Ph.D.s in fields such as the sciences choose to go into industry rather than academia. In chemistry, for example, about 65 percent of students go into industry, approximately three times the number that choose four-year colleges or universities (Presidential Task Force 1995). When these considerations are taken into account, the numbers of PFF participants are more encouraging.

Further, doctoral education is largely carried out at the department level, and changes need to be made one department at a time. PFF leaders have gradually expanded the number of departments that are involved. The Arizona State University program started in 1994, with twenty-five students from five departments., and by 1998–1999 it involved 105 students and thirty-one of the forty-six doctoral programs. Despite significant growth, leaders are seeking additional ways for PFF to have even greater impact. In the Arizona State example, the provost urged PFF leaders to take steps to reach even more students. They developed an action plan with the following components:

◆ PFF presentations at department meetings

◆ A PFF fellow in each department to serve as point person to organize PFF-like activities with the graduate student organization in the department

◆ A PFF lecture series planned and executed by the PFF first-year participants for all graduate students and faculty in the department

◆ ASU mentors, where appropriate, involved as PFF participants go out to the partner institutions

◆ New faculty who demonstrate potential for positive PFF participation

◆ Job announcements forwarded from the national PFF office to relevant chairs and directors of graduate doctoral studies as well as to PFF fellows

◆ Upcoming PFF projects announced and graduate faculty invited to become involved where interest is indicated

◆ Articles and updates on PFF activities written for departmental newsletters.

It is clear that leaders of PFF initiatives are envisioning a new way to conduct doctoral study, not just a curious sideshow.

Other universities in the national PFF program are experiencing similar growth. For example, the University of Minnesota in 1998 enrolled about 210 students in its two-course PFF program; it has involved students in seventy-seven of its 110 doctoral programs, and has recruited over 294 faculty mentors in twelve partner institutions. Syracuse University has graduated, from virtually every department, 120 individuals who have been involved in its Future Professoriate Project, and it has over 200 trained teaching mentors. It has awarded eighty Certificates in University Teaching and has 134 professional portfolios on file. From working with five departments in 1994–1995, Howard University by 1998–1999 involves seventeen of twenty-six doctoral departments in its Graduate School of Arts and Sciences. Florida State University started with four departments and currently has expanded to ten. Indiana University started with three, and currently has nine.

From a curious novelty involving only a few students, faculty members, and departments, PFF programs are moving to the preferred way to prepare for a career in the academy. Those involved have seen the benefits first hand and have become strong advocates for expanding the numbers of students, faculty members, and departments. Growth has occurred, but if PFF is to become the norm rather than the exception, further expansion is required. When PFF becomes normative and traditional programs the exception, then we are confident that PFF will prevail—at least until a better way is devised.

4. Changing institutional practices. Colleges and universities are complex social systems, and changes in one part impact other parts of the organization. When an innovation is introduced in one part of the system, policies and practices in place to support other activities must be revised so that they, at the very least, do not undermine it. Ideally, the other policies and practices would be modified in order to institutionalize the new approach, in ways described below. PFF programs should strive to create linkages with developments elsewhere, such as setting institutional policies and doing strategic planning. Moreover, new programs often accentuate the need for additional changes, such as creation of career planning and placement services, all of which contribute to the institutionalization of the program.

Policies that support PFF programs are needed. For instance, the faculty in the Howard University Graduate School of Arts and Sciences voted unanimously to make PFF a top priority. This had the effect of empowering the graduate dean to allocate budget to support PFF and to seek external funding.

In addition, Howard is linking its Graduate Assistance in Areas of National Need (GAANN) program (that supports undergraduates interested in graduate education) to PFF and involving GAANN in some of the PFF activities. Similarly, the graduate faculty at Emory University requires students in all doctoral programs to participate in its Teaching Assistant Training and Teaching Opportunities program. It is a four-step program involving: 1) a summer workshop on basic teaching skills and methods, 2) a course in discipline-specific teaching problems and strategies, 3) monitored first-teaching opportunities as a teaching assistant, and 4) co-teaching a course as a teaching associate with a faculty member. Policies like these are evidence of strong institutional support for more comprehensive preparation.

Strategic planning is another arena which can provide support for PFF. The University of Kentucky has developed a new strategic plan, and among other things, it states, "All departments will have a teaching assistant development/ Preparing Future Faculty plan." Linda Worley, director of the PFF initiative, writes, "This is a major help in institutionalizing the PFF projects, since the language and spirit are now embedded in the university's five-year plan." Arizona State has identified PFF as a major initiative in their "university for the next century" capital campaign.

Unlike undergraduate education, where career planning and placement services are widely available, doctoral education has left career matters to students and their advisors (Pruitt and Issacs 1997). Recognizing the serious problems that individuals with new doctorates are encountering in gaining suitable employment, a few universities are creating new positions to work with potential employers, to call attention to the talents of their doctoral students and recent graduates, and to assist students in securing faculty appointments. For example, Arizona State University assigned an associate dean to develop student support services in the graduate school, and University of Notre Dame created the position of director of career services and placement devoted specifically to its graduate school. Both individuals are trying to create more job opportunities, generate internships and other experiences to link students with employers and explore alternative careers for graduates. Because PFF programs are giving students sophistication about faculty roles and about institutional differences that prepare them for a variety of academic jobs, they are encouraging other academic leaders to focus on career planning and preparation.

5. *Providing financial support.* Failing to make the transition from grant support to institutional support is perhaps the most common reason for the failure of innovations that are supported by external funds. But, virtually all PFF leaders acknowledge that these programs do not require a great deal of money.

The vision, the ideas, and their champions are crucial to sustaining new faculty preparation programs, and they are the ingredients for garnering the necessary resources.

Nonetheless, financial support is needed, and the national PFF program has taken several steps to make this transition easier. First, we should be clear about the amount of grant support that was available to support the clusters. In Phase I, five clusters were awarded grants of $170,000 over a two-year period to develop model programs. We established two conditions that allowed grant dollars to go further than they might otherwise have: 1) they were not to be used for student stipends (the program is intended as a professional development initiative and not a support program), and 2) they were not to be used for faculty salaries. The clusters spent their money only for program activities.

The other twelve clusters in Phase I were awarded grants of just $10,000 and encouraged to participate over the two years in meetings, publications, listservs, presentations, etc., thereby becoming full partners in the development of the intellectual capital of PFF. This meant that these twelve clusters had to use their own resources to support their incipient PFF programs. Although all universities provided a substantial match to their grants, these twelve universities actually invested far more of their own funds than they received, using the grant and involvement in the national initiative as justification for institutional funds. All twelve accomplished a great deal, in many cases not qualitatively different from those with more funding, although few were able to match the larger funded initiative in terms of the size of programs or numbers of participants. In fact, five of the twelve were selected to participate in the second phase precisely because they had accomplished so much using their own funds. For these institutions there was no need for weaning from grant support. Indeed, Professor Thomas Rischel who directs the PFF program in the department of mathematics at Cornell University argues cogently that it is easier to sustain a small program with limited outside funds than it is a large program developed with sizable grants. He reports that the modest support to sustain his program has been provided by the administration and is now institutionalized—at least in budgetary terms.

During Phase II, grants of $20,000 per year for three years are awarded to each of the fifteen clusters. As anyone experienced in education knows, these are not large sums. Again, institutions are investing far more of their own resources to support PFF programs than they are receiving in grants. The institutional funding is provided because by now the leaders have been able to observe the benefits of these new ways to prepare future professors.

That having been said, campus leaders still need to budget for PFF programs and for their growth. How are clusters doing that? In the same ways that other academic programs are supported: through a combination of sources, including funds from the graduate school, departments, tuition, endowment, teaching-learning center, and special appeals. For example, PFF courses not only encapsulate and regularize the learning process, they can also generate tuition dollars. The Universities of Minnesota and New Hampshire use tuition revenue to partially support their PFF programs. The University of Washington has received a substantial gift, which was placed in a permanent endowment to fund students and their faculty mentors to do significant instructional improvement projects following the PFF model. However these programs are funded, they require a stable resource base if they are to continue the current pattern of growth, expansion, and quality.

Huckabay Fellows Program
University of Washington

In 1995 the University of Washington established an endowment for fellowships. Inspired by PFF, these fellowships were designated to fund students seeking to enhance their preparation as teachers, rather than for traditional research awards. Each Huckabay Fellow designed and carried out a project dealing with teaching and learning, working with a faculty collaborator either from the university or from another campus. In the first competition nine were selected from among sixty-seven applications. Quarter-long projects spanned the academic disciplines and included such diverse efforts as:

◆ astronomy revising the introductory survey course to focus on current cutting edge research topics;

◆ teaching English literature by infusing feminist perspectives in a community college; and

◆ nursing revising a required course on populations at risk by drawing on interdisciplinary perspectives, using computers, and incorporating active and collaborative means of learning.

Indiana University is able to use funds generated by research grants to support departments experimenting with new models of PFF. In addition, President Myles Brand developed a strategic plan for the system, set aside a substantial budget, and requested proposals from throughout the system. A PFF-inspired initiative called Future Faculty Teaching Fellowships sends advanced doctoral students to teach at one of the system's seven non-residential branch campuses for a semester or year. The program includes an orientation to teaching and provides strong mentoring and support for the professional development of the Fellows.

Promoting Inclusiveness

Despite gains in recent years, the faculties of colleges and universities as well as doctoral students in the pipeline remain overwhelmingly white. Predictions are that one-third of the nation will be ethnic or racial minorities by the turn of the century, yet only about ten percent of faculty are persons of color. At this time, the academic profession, facing a turnover of large numbers of faculty members, has an opportunity to shape the future faculty to look more like America and more like the increasingly diverse student population. It has an opportunity as well to exercise leadership with respect to human equality. Moreover, colleges and universities are faced with pressure to diversify the pool of candidates who are available for new assistant professor positions.

To enhance minority participation in graduate education, the Council of Graduate Schools adopted in 1997 a statement on inclusiveness *Building an Inclusive Graduate Community: A Statement of Principles.* This document reaffirms the belief those seeking talented students from groups historically underrepresented in graduate education and encouraging them to pursue advanced degrees serve the best interests of higher education and the nation at large.

There are substantial challenges inherent in diversifying the faculty and strengthening the ability of future faculty to teach diverse students. Faculty preparation is being conducted in a climate that eschews affirmative action, witnesses a rise in hate crimes, and where people the world over consciously exclude or devalue certain groups of people. Biases that permeate society are reflected in the actions of faculty and students. We believe, however, that the faculty of the future must understand how discrimination affects the learning environment in higher education. Thus, it is incumbent upon PFF to play a major role in diversifying the faculty and strengthening the ability of future faculty to teach diverse students.

1. Diversifying the Faculty. Underrepresented on college and university faculties are African Americans, Asian or Pacific Islanders, Chicanos, Latinos, or Hispanics, and American Indian or Alaskan Natives. We learned from our surveys of PFF participants in 1995 and 1996 that PFF student participation mirrors the same underrepresentation. Unfortunately, this means that PFF is failing to increase the number of minorities in the future faculty pipeline. A challenge to PFF programs is to recruit more doctoral students from these groups.

In response, PFF programs must make special efforts to point out to all underrepresented students the importance of the professoriate and encourage doctoral students to enroll. Program faculty should identify promising undergraduate students early and give them opportunities to teach and conduct research, thus introducing them to academic careers.

PFF responses at the national level include forming alliances for enhancing diversity in the professorial pipeline by collaborating with such groups as Compact for Faculty Diversity, Ronald E. McNair Postbaccalaureate Achievement Program, McKnight Doctoral Fellowship Program in Florida, National Black Graduate Student Association, and Consortium for Developing Historically Black College and University New Faculty. PFF is helping to develop a manual for recruiting faculty of color in collaboration with the AAC&U project on American Commitments: Diversity, Democracy and Liberal Learning, a project involving scores of campuses to address diversity in classrooms, the campus, and community. The third phase of PFF, involving the sciences and mathematics, emphasizes this pipeline concern. Criteria for selecting science and mathematics departments for participation require the departments to supply information about racial and ethnic representation among their students, and, perhaps more importantly, state their plans for the future.

Although efforts like these at the national level are necessary, they are not sufficient. At the cluster level, for example, the Graduate Dean at Howard University makes it a practice to include required PFF participation in proposals to secure funding for doctoral preparation. Howard has received a grant of $1 million from the Lilly Endowment/UNCF Historically Black Colleges and Universities Program that supports the development of a new doctoral scholars program. It is designed to increase the number of Ph.D. recipients among African Americans and individuals from other underrepresented groups who wish to pursue a teaching career in higher education. Another example is Howard's NSF/Minorities in Graduate Education Project. This is an intensive summer research program that requires participation in the PFF program and a rigorous mentoring and retention program for science, mathematics, and engineering majors.

At Northwestern University the Department of Materials Science is recruiting minority students through an NSF grant to address issues of diversity and to prepare minority students for careers as teachers of science.

We engaged PFF participants at our summer 1999 conference in thinking about ways that PFF could respond to the challenge of diversifying the faculty. One comment summarizes our discussion: "We cannot diversify the faculty quickly enough. We must re-educate the existing faculty to understand issues of difference and to be able to work with these differences. It is everyone's re-

Meeting the Future Challenges of PFF: How Shall We Work to Diversify the Faculty?

S elected comments came from brainstorming sessions at the 1999 PFF summer conference during which best and new ideas were sought.

1. Explore ways PFF can work to help undergraduates and graduates come to view faculty careers as desirable and possible.

2. Work with other campus groups (e.g., Women in Science and Engineering).

3. Reach out to minority students at junior and sophomore levels.

4. PFF is an excellent tool for diversifying the faculty. As we aggressively work to diversify PFF and work to ensure that more students complete their doctoral programs, they will move on to faculty positions.

5. Grow your own Ph.D. students of color into the faculty of your department.

6. Focus as much on retention as on hiring. Ask under-represented groups of faculty what they need to feel comfortable and productive in their new positions—then provide it.

7. Encourage graduating doctoral students to remind the administration that we are aware of the weakness of the existing faculty pool in terms of their lack of diversity.

8. Extend the definition of minority/diversity to include international students so that they can participate in federally funded programs aimed at increasing the involvement of such students.

9. Work on retention of underrepresented groups in graduate programs.

sponsibility to do so. From the PFF student to the administrators we must take the lead. PFF may be the best mechanism to do this!"

2. Developing Capacities to Teach Diverse Students. A concern that is related to the weak representation of minorities in PFF is the relatively weak impact that PFF programs seem to be having on the ability of participants to deal with diversity. In our surveys of PFF students, developing the ability to deal with a diversity of students was ranked lowest on the list of benefits of participation in PFF. More nonwhite than white participants reported that their PFF experiences improved their ability to be successful with diverse students "quite a lot" or "very much." We interpret this response to indicate that more work is necessary within the program to assist future faculty in understanding the implications of rapidly changing student demographics.

This awareness of the gap between potential and reality led us to include, as a special focus in PFF Phase II, effectiveness in bringing about inclusive educational practice, that is, approaches to education that are welcoming to students from all social groups. These approaches involve both pedagogy and curricular choices. Pedagogy focuses on the *what* of teaching—the content; the second on the *how*—the teaching methods. PFF students must become adept at choosing printed and audiovisual materials, and in selecting topics, assignments, and research projects that value the wide variety of perspectives and interests that exist among their students. In like manner they must learn teaching methods and interpersonal approaches that reflect genuine respect for and understanding of the heterogeneous mix of students that populate higher education.

The clusters are holding workshops and seminars on these matters and involving partner institutions as laboratories. Some are making efforts to help participants to be reflective about their own biases and to examine their own thoughts and actions. At partner campuses PFF participants are talking with learners from previously underrepresented groups and learning about their backgrounds, their values and their motivation. One PFF participant related how pleased she was when she had the opportunity to examine curricula, syllabi, and text materials with her mentor and revise these materials to eliminate overt bias. Together they authored a paper on this topic. Experiences like these are effective ways to help faculty in their efforts to encourage the success of all students (Chism and Pruitt 1995).

Clusters employ a variety of strategies to provide these experiences. Arizona State University, for example, has set as a priority a focus on diversity throughout the PFF seminars. They distributed readings throughout the year that relate the seminar topic to diversity issues. They added a companion seminar to one on "Teaching in the Inclusive Classroom." It focuses on the research agenda, with the idea of engaging a more diverse group of faculty, graduate students, and undergraduates in research funding opportunities. The panel was given by the vice provost for research, a faculty member who has headed up funding in the sciences for underrepresented groups in both higher and secondary education, and a faculty member who has brought in substantial research funding for Hispanic faculty and graduate students across disciplines.

Northwestern University continues to work with its cluster partner, Chicago State University, to create programs that allow them to talk about the way white teachers have altered their materials in order to be more effective teachers of African American students. PFF students at Northwestern seek advice from African American faculty and students regarding curriculum, selection of materials, and the role of the community and church in education.

Syracuse and Howard Universities have created a relationship that enables them to visit each other's campuses so that PFF students can interact with each other and with their undergraduates, and learn what it is like to be a faculty

Meeting the Future Challenges of PFF: How Shall We Work to Develop the Capacity to Teach Diverse Students?

Selected comments came from brainstorming sessions at the 1999 PFF summer conference during which best and new ideas were sought.

1. Doctoral students in PFF groups share strategies for teaching and research in the inclusive classroom and laboratory.

2. Train graduate students in mentoring skills (especially in issues of diversity) and give them opportunities to mentor undergraduates from diverse institutions.

3. Partner with cluster campuses, which are strong in adult/continuing education.

4. Expose PFF students and mentors to various learning styles (possibly through joint participation in the PFF participation courses).

5. Ensure that that PFF graduate student interact with undergraduates of as many different types of institutions as possible.

6. Enlist members of programs that deal with undergraduate programs such as McNair and educational opportunity programs to serve as "experts" in diversity issues.

7. Teach communication skills for a diverse classroom.

8. Prepare PFF participants to consider every student's diversity at all times, and then underrepresented groups of undergraduates will usually benefit.

9. Hold skits/role playing of hypothetical situations followed by discussion of how to deal with each case.

10. Observe classes and meet students at cluster institutions to learn about the different types of diversity.

11. Hold discussion groups of teaching assistants and faculty who are currently teaching to discuss diversity issues that have come up.

12. There are so many ways in which we are diverse. A first and important step is to provide opportunities to dialogue (PFF students and those who are different) so that graduate students become more sensitive to different needs, experiences, etc.

member at historically black or at predominantly white campuses. The University of New Hampshire and Howard have also started similar intervisitation. To expand opportunities to learn about and from a wide range of students, University of New Hampshire included UNH at Manchester—a predominantly two-year, urban, nontraditional, commuter campus, located in the state's most ethnically diverse population—as a partner.

Other examples of outreach to institutions with racially and ethnically distinctive student bodies include partnering between Duke and North Carolina Central Universities, and the University of Nebraska and Grambling State University. Nebraska recruited the two most diverse academic institutions in Nebraska as partners: Metropolitan Community College and University of Nebraska-Omaha. Nebraska also created relationships with distance partners such as Grambling, an historically black university, and they plan to work next year with New Mexico Highlands, an Hispanic- and Native American-serving institution, and Texas A & M-Corpus Christi, an Hispanic-serving institution.

When queried about what they would do to deepen expertise in work with diverse students, participants at the 1999 summer conference said they would, for instance, arrange sessions so that faculty and students from diverse groups could exchange roles, that is, "walk in the other's shoes." They would train graduate students in mentoring skills and give them opportunities to mentor undergraduates from diverse institutions. One participant summed up the challenge by saying that it is important to prepare PFF participants to consider every student's diversity at all times.

A great deal is known about addressing diversity of students in the curriculum, teaching and learning approaches, and institutional climate (see, for example <http://www.diversityweb.org>) and PFF programs must continue to connect faculty and future faculty with this information.

Changing the "Culture of Faculty Preparation"

Our long term goal is to improve the quality of undergraduate education by changing the way graduate schools prepare students to become professors. Achieving this goal requires changes in the academy that far transcend the work of the PFF clusters. Much work needs to be done beyond the active clusters, and AAC&U and CGS are using their good offices—and their memberships—to advance the goal of changing the "culture of preparation." Below are a number of strategies being pursued.

1. Spreading PFF to other institutions. If the culture is to change, more than the current clusters must become players. We have learned of many other institutions developing similar programs. Categories of similar initiatives include:

◆ Several universities have developed their own versions of PFF programs, usually with a focus on teaching and without the use of partners. University of California, Irvine, University of Utah, and University of Wyoming are examples.

◆ Some new PFF programs are in the early stages of development; for example, in one state, The University of Michigan, Western Michigan University, Michigan State University, and Wayne State University are in various stages of developing programs. Virginia Commonwealth University is developing a program with a special focus on preparing professors for professional fields.

◆ During the 1960s and 1970s a new degree was developed, the Doctor of Arts, as a means to prepare college professors. Although the degree did not catch on as its advocates wanted, several universities still operate these programs. The programs at Idaho State University and Ball State University have affinity with the purposes and values of PFF programs.

◆ Although PFF has focused on doctoral education, a similar need exists for masters programs that prepare faculty to teach in community colleges. Community colleges grew dramatically during the 1960s and 1970s, as the nation created, for a time, an average of a college a week. The faculties that were hired to staff those new colleges are starting to retire, and large numbers of new faculty will be hired. Studies by Hammonds (1998) indicate that almost all of the recent hires have been individuals with a masters degree in their subjects and with teaching experience. Assuming this trend continues, there will be a need for PFF programs specifically for students seeking to work in two-year colleges. Already the University of Arkansas has developed such a pilot program, as has the communications department at Eastern Michigan University, with support from the National Communications Association. The developmnent of PFF programs at comprehensive institutions offering masters degrees is an emerging growth area for PFF. One might expect that the faculty members at masters institutions would be more eager to embrace PFF concepts and practices than the faculty at research universities.

◆ PFF-like programs are developing internationally. Several Canadian universities have certificate programs in university teaching. Universities at Guelph, Manitoba, New Brunswick, Saskatchewan, and York are examples. We have learned of interest in PFF from universities in countries as diverse as Brazil, England, France, India, Austria, and Spain.

Various PFF clusters are taking responsibility for spreading the word to other institutions. The University of Colorado held a state-wide conference that brought different institutions together to build networks of collaboration for PFF.

Indiana University held a system-wide conference called "PFF on a Shoestring: Keeping the Programs When Funding Runs Out." The University of Cincinnati held a regional conference for academic leaders from Indiana, Kentucky, and Ohio. And many individuals have made presentations about PFF ideas and experiences in their professional associations.

Although the PFF ideas are spreading rapidly — independently of PFF — and leaders at other universities are devising similar programs, many more campuses need to actively support the PFF agenda before such preparation becomes the standard for aspiring academics.

2. Developing more respect for professional standards. Large bodies of research literature exist on effectiveness of different approaches to teaching (McKeachie 1998; Menges, Weimer, and Associates 1996), learning (Chickering and Gamson 1991), impact of college on students (Pascarella and Terenzini 1991), student evaluation of teaching (Marsh and Dunkin 1992), and curriculum (Gaff and Ratcliff 1996), among others. Few faculty are aware of this literature and the value that it may offer to their professional work. Moreover, many dismiss this work as "educationist," because it seems less worthy than the substance of their fields. It is time to acknowledge that professors can learn a great deal about their professional practices from this kind of scholarly work and to establish expectations that professionals should be acquainted with the resources that this work provides.

Similarly, in the matter of service, it is time to return to fundamentals. During earlier decades of the twentieth century, faculty members struggled against the church, the state, boards of trustees, and administrations to gain a legitimate role in the shared governance of colleges and universities. Based on their *expert authority* rather than *bureaucratic authority*, faculty members now have primary authority over the instructional program. Specifically, they are responsible in large part for designing and approving the curriculum and individual courses, because, for example, only a physicist knows what a physicist needs to know. Similarly, they have primary authority in the hiring and promotion of their colleagues, based on their qualifications as a scholar. In addition, faculty have a right and responsibility to participate in other decisions affecting the institution. It is curious that faculty have never been formally trained for any of these responsibilities. If faculty are to exercise their authority over the instructional program, and if they are to consult usefully about other institutional matters, learning how modern institutions operate and developing at least a modicum of expertise about strategic planning, managing finances, fund raising, and conducting public relations are requisites.

At one time, the talented amateur may have sufficed for teaching and for participating in shared governance, but today higher standards are needed for professional practice in teaching and service to match the high standards in place for research.

3. Changing attitudes and practices throughout the academy. It is one thing to change a few institutional practices at a few clusters and quite another for major structural features of the academy to honor those changes and incorporate them into their regular practices. We have already noted that *learned societies* are now working to develop PFF programs in doctoral departments around the country. We anticipate that these pilot projects will generate greater understanding and support for the new kinds of preparation we envision. Administrators of *graduate fellowships*, we believe, should write award guidelines that require the more comprehensive education provided by PFF programs. Syracuse University has already shown the feasibility of this approach. In the traditional pattern, a university identifies the "best and brightest" doctoral students to receive fellowships that financially support their education, freeing them from assistantships and other jobs as a means of financial support, so they may concentrate full time on their studies. However, hearing about their peers in the Future Professoriate Project, the fellows requested the professional development opportunities it provided, and, specifically, the opportunity to teach, work with a teaching mentor, and develop a professional portfolio.

Administrators of graduate fellowships would do well to heed this experience and, rather than separating students from enriching professional experiences with others, write fellowship guidelines that include educational PFF experiences and opportunities to interact with students in their own and other departments and with faculty members in other institutions.

A major new fellowship program operated by the Southern Regional Education Board enacts such professional development. As part of a larger Compact for Faculty Diversity, it provides five years of fellowship aid to minority students pursuing doctorate degrees. Universities, and often states, must sign agreements not only to provide funding but also to include mentoring, professional development, and assistance in developing a professional portfolio for the fellows. Nearly 300 fellows have been funded under this more robust approach.

Postdoctorate positions, primarily in the sciences, were once seen as preparation for an academic job. Postdoctorate fellows do build their credentials in research, but they get little added experience in the teaching or service that would make them more marketable as faculty members. A report on the job market in fourteen different scientific disciplines (AAAS 1998) indicates that more than half of the recent Ph.D.s in chemistry, physics, and earth and space sciences held temporary jobs, and more than half of those said they did so "involuntarily," that is, because they could not find suitable permanent positions. In the life sciences, for example, there are an estimated 20,000 postdoctoral fellows, and "recent graduates have found themselves in a 'holding pattern'" (NAS 1998, p. 3). In 1995, fully 38 percent were still in temporary positions five to six years after getting their degrees (NAS 1998). What this army of postdocs, and those who support them, need to know is that most institutions hiring faculty expect them to do more than conduct research; fellows need broader experience characteristic of new faculty preparation programs to develop the balanced portfolio of qualities frequently sought by colleges and universities. An example of the kind of program we have in mind is the Postdoctoral Fellowships in Science, Mathematics, Engineering, and Technological Education at the National Science Foundation (1998), providing support for both research and education.

Modest adjustments in the normal operating procedures of the learned societies, fellowship funders, and providers of postdoctorate fellowships — key parts of the infrastructure of doctoral study — would go a long way toward enhancing the preparation of future faculty.

4. Stimulating a market demand for better prepared faculty. As a rule, educational associations operate programs that help institutions to create model programs, featuring their innovations in publications and meetings, and hoping that others will learn and adapt some of their features. This is only part of the PFF strategy; we think that is insufficient. We believe that the PFF experience should have value in the marketplace and that institutions hiring new faculty ought to place a premium on PFF learning.

We have taken a number of steps to stimulate a market demand for comprehensively educated faculty members described in this report. These steps involve bringing information about the availability of professionally prepared doctorate holders to hiring officials, and information about the needs of hiring institutions to students in preparation programs. We are publishing an essay to be distributed widely to graduate faculty that articulates the expectations for new faculty hired by the vast majority of colleges and universities. These are not research universities, and their missions and faculty roles are quite different from those of doctoral universities. These other institutions vary enormously, but, generally, in order to be hired and to succeed in them, candidates are expected to possess the following qualities.

◆ *Teaching ability.* To be sure, successful teaching experience is expected of new faculty, as is the capacity to contribute to new initiatives in the undergraduate curriculum (e.g., writing, diversity, and interdisciplinary programs), to use engaging approaches to teaching and learning (e.g., technological, collaborative, and service learning), and to teach and advise a diversity of students.

◆ *Research productivity.* Although expectations for research vary widely, all faculty are expected to keep up with their discipline. Many institutions require research and publication, emphasize the development of a research program that fits with other responsibilities, and the involvement of undergraduate students in research.

◆ *Involvement in academic life.* Involvements also vary from institution to institution, but most expect new faculty members to bring new intellectual vitality and educational programming to their departments and to contribute to the academic community. Some colleges expect faculty to participate in community events and to carry out the institution's mission in their teaching and research.

We expect that this kind of information will help graduate faculty members become more aware of the need for more comprehensive preparation than has been usual.

In addition, we helped support a study (Benasi and Seidel 1999) of the hiring practices of a large number of colleges and universities to assess the possibility that PFF experiences might add value to the doctoral experience. Chairs that hired faculty members in the last three years indicated that they valued teaching capacity highly in the search process, but faculty members who were hired reported that little documentation was requested of them by the search committees. Some faculty members, many of them from PFF institutions, voluntarily sent statements of teaching interests, statements of a teaching philosophy, student evaluations of their teaching, or portfolios of their work. In each instance, the chairs regarded these materials as more important in the hiring decision than did the candidate. It appears that hiring institutions are less demanding of candidates than they might be and that they could improve their success by requiring more documentation of the qualities expected of faculty members.

If the PFF experience is actually as valuable as envisioned, the academic job market will eventually reflect that. To understand that market and help it work more efficiently by providing information about the jobs and those preparing for them is one of our objectives.

5. Turning PFF alumni into a national resource. Hundreds of new doctorates are becoming alumni with PFF experience, and thereby a valuable resource. Not only are they at the cutting edge regarding research and methodologies in their disciplines, they also are, in many ways, more attuned to professional expectations and resources in the areas of teaching and service than their senior colleagues. How can this growing sociological phenomenon be used to improve the professoriate and advance the quality of undergraduate education?

This question has not yet been answered, but we envision the possibility of creating a national network similar to the Danforth postgraduates of an earlier time. The Danforth Foundation awarded graduate fellowships that included emphases on interdisciplinary, value-related education, and those who completed their degrees were encouraged to attend periodic gatherings to discuss teaching and professional issues. In addition, a number of faculty members were designated as Danforth Associates and were funded to hold special activities with undergraduate students outside of class. In a similar way, as the number of PFF alumni grows, so does the potential for enlisting them for the continuing effort to improve the quality of a college education and strengthen academic institutions.

6. Maintaining a national office. Even after the grants supporting PFF programs end, we will need an office to advocate for PFF programs, connect them with other national initiatives, encourage assessment and research into their long term benefits, and support the work of individual clusters. In evaluating Phase I of PFF for The Pew Charitable Trusts, Jon Wergin, Virginia Commonwealth University expert on the process of educational change, commented that academic change is furthered most by a determination to stay with an innovation for a substantial period of time. He argues that long term persistence is more important than the size of grants or the number of foundation grant awards. Although no specific plans are in place at this time, we can assert that AAC&U and CGS are committed to seeing the success of PFF and will continue to provide national leadership for this endeavor for the foreseeable future.

In conclusion, academic leaders at existing clusters are building the foundations to sustain the new preparation programs when grant support ends and to further diversify the faculty. We have made a good start at transforming the culture of preparation of future faculty. While the final chapter on this matter is yet to be written, and although we know that change in the academic culture is a slow and uncertain venture, a good deal of momentum has been generated, and prospects are promising.

CHAPTER 5

Conclusions and Action Recommendations

The most highly regarded groups of academics in the country, including major constituencies of doctoral education, have called for a fundamental realignment of faculty work and a revision of doctoral study to support new definitions of academic work.

◆ The National Academy of Science, National Academy of Engineering, and National Institute of Medicine issued a joint report (COSEPUP 1995) calling for a "new Ph. D. degree," one that cultivates a broader range of academic and career skills, offers more program options, provides students with greater knowledge about alternative careers, and fosters a greater sense of entrepreneurship.

◆ The Association of American Universities, comprised of sixty-two leading universities that produce over half of all doctorates awarded annually, issued a report (1998) that declared, "Student interests should be paramount in designing a graduate curriculum that prepares students for a broad array of careers," and that "if student interests become subsidiary to conflicting institutional or faculty interests, the educational benefits of . . . apprenticeship arrangements can be undermined" (p. 17). It went on to discuss a set of best practices, citing PFF as "one of the most systematic efforts to increase graduate student preparation for teaching" (p. 21).

◆ The Presidential Young Investigators, the best and brightest young science researchers, issued a startling report (1991) that called for greater emphasis on teaching at their universities. Specifically, they recommended that U.S. higher education "encourage and reward teaching excellence, instructional scholarship, and public service as well as research" (p. 10).

◆ In a major national study of persons who had received doctorates ten to thirteen years earlier, Cerney and Nerad (1997) reported that from 30–41 percent of those in a variety of disciplines confessed to never having received information from graduate faculty about finding jobs. Others said that teamwork, interdisciplinary capacities, and organizational skills were important for their jobs but that little attention had been given to any of these in their doctoral programs. In an open-ended question about suggestions for improving doctoral programs, many English scholars cited more realistic career information and learning how to teach, while many biochemists mentioned grantsmanship and communications skills as areas for improvement.

◆ The National Association of Graduate and Professional Students, (General Session Bill GS- 96-5), voted unanimously to adopt a resolution endorsing the PFF "philosophy and objectives relating to pedagogical skill building (e.g., learning styles, assessment and teaching philosophies) and professional development (e.g., rank and tenure, job search, and interview)." They also urged that student achievement in these areas be acknowledged by their department and university through such means as course credit, certificate, or notation on transcript.

Is the system that we have created impervious to change, even at the urging of our most thoughtful academic leaders?

A remarkable convergence emerges in the analyses and recommendations of these crucial constituencies of doctoral education: eminent science, medicine, and engineering academies, leading research universities, accomplished young scientific researchers, holders of doctoral degrees, and graduate students. Since their rhetoric coincides, one question must be why their recommendations have not found their way into the mainstream of practice in doctoral education. All these groups are calling for significant change, but little is changing. Is the system that we have created impervious to change, even at the urging of our most thoughtful academic leaders?

Preparing Future Faculty as a Strategy for Organizational Change

PFF involves specific strategies that already reflect these recommendations for change in academic institutions. PFF, as a meaningful and practical catalyst for change in the structure and culture of the academy, can effectively prepare future generations for the actual work performed by college and university professors.

We have learned many lessons since 1993. Here are a few of the most important:

◆ Virtually all of the PFF programs appear to be successful, suggesting that the animating PFF ideas are sound and adaptable to particular contexts.

◆ It is possible to overcome the legal autonomy and competitive relationships among colleges and universities to create new forms of institutional collaboration for preparing the future professoriate.

◆ New forms of mentoring for teaching and service can be a fruitful complement to mentoring for research.

◆ Graduate students are eager to be treated like junior faculty and work closely with faculty colleagues in partner institutions.

◆ Partner faculty members enjoy working with doctoral students and derive many benefits that stimulate their own professional development.

◆ An increasing number of graduate faculty appreciate the opportunity that PFF gives their students to better prepare themselves for academic positions, even though it involves a shift from more traditional approaches.

◆ PFF programs provide significant benefits to departments and universities that offer them, such as the kinds of academic involvement associated with recruitment and retention of talented students.

◆ Interest in faculty preparation programs is growing among leaders throughout doctoral education, and many universities are creating their own programs with their own funds.

◆ Changing the culture of doctoral preparation is a difficult, slow, and uneven process, but significant gains can be seen after only a few years, as educational associations, learned societies, funding agencies, and other organizations weigh in to support PFF ideas and practices.

Our Vision of the Faculty We Need

Integration of Teaching, Research, and Service. Our vision of the faculty we need demands integration of teaching, research, and service. At its best, the American professoriate is composed of professionals who are excellent teachers and productive researchers who, like other professionals, serve their institutions, professional organizations, and communities. Although the definitions of teaching, research, and service may vary, and the balance among these three responsibilities may differ at different institutions and at different times in an academic career, all three are integral to the faculty job. Academics need to receive graduate preparation that encompasses all three, and throughout their careers, we believe, faculty need to develop greater sophistication in each, continuously seeking to balance and integrate these responsibilities in ways that are both individually fulfilling and that serve the needs of their students and institutions. PFF programs are proving to be practical ways to provide broader, more holistic preparation for academic careers.

> We think that the academy should hold a larger and more holistic vision of faculty intellectual work and should insist that faculty play a genuine role in governing academic institutions.

Our vision of the faculty we need in the future differs in important ways from today's trends. A worrisome tendency is for specific faculty responsibilities to be carved up and for institutions to contract with individuals to do specific tasks—teach lower division courses, design courses to be offered electronically, or to conduct research projects. Another is for faculty to be removed from a meaningful role in the shared governance of their institutions, as activist boards, professionalized administrations, and market pressures requiring nimble responses are more prominent. Although the faculty itself has contributed to these conditions, we think that the academy should hold a larger and more holistic vision of faculty intellectual work and should insist that faculty play a genuine role in governing academic institutions. These agendas ought to be addressed in the graduate preparation of faculty, and then continued throughout academic careers.

The faculty ranks today are populated by growing numbers of part-time, adjunct, and temporary positions. These faculty members are specifically contracted to teach and not to do research or provide service. These employees are seldom integrated into the lives of their departments, let alone asked to participate in decisions affecting the unit or institution. The decision to increase the use of temporary faculty is primarily an effort to reduce the cost of instruction, as salaries and benefits tend to be lower than for full-time faculty.

PFF programs endeavor to restore respect for the fullness of college professor's work, precisely because it has at its heart not teaching, not research, nor service but the *integration* of teaching, research, and service. PFF helps clarify for the public, and even for the faculty themselves, the absolute value of what Jane Tompkins (1996) wrote about so passionately: whole professors advancing the holistic education of students. Effective faculty are central to any conception of effective education or effective institutions. In terms of their educational and institutional value, there is no comparison between full-time, permanent faculty members who are excellent teachers, effective researchers, and committed to serve their communities, and a parade of "partial professionals" who, however effective they may be in doing a particular task, can have little educational or institutional impact because of the structure of their positions. Leaders of the PFF initiative seek to develop individuals who can integrate teaching, research, and service to be full professionals, thus, full-time faculty. We urge greater reliance on full-time faculty devoted to the best that has characterized the professoriate—and more effective preparation of faculty, so they can do those jobs.

Emphasis on Institutional Contexts. In their doctoral education, faculty members are primarily socialized into a discipline, not a profession. The emphasis is almost exclusively on cutting edge intellectual, theoretical, empirical, and methodological content of a field of study, with the operating assumption, often unstated, that once an individual masters a specialization, s/he can practice it by teaching or conducting research in any of a number of organizational contexts. For faculty members, the disciplines provide primary professional identities, promote their particular perspectives and interests, claim loyalties, and even offer career pathways. Disciplinary specialization is so central to doctoral education that it has become, at some level, hostile to its institutional home. Yet, *it is institutions, not disciplines*, that create jobs, hire individuals, define their work assignments, evaluate their effectiveness, give promotions and salary increases, and support the professional development and career progress of faculty. The overemphasis on academic disciplines and underemphasis on the institutions in which the discipline is practiced unwittingly conspire against the creation of faculty positions that require more complete professionals.

PFF cultivates institutional perspectives, interests, responsibilities, and loyalties by focusing on the variety of academic institutions where graduates might find satisfying work. As such, it provides a balance between institutional and disciplinary loyalties. It provides graduate students with direct experience with different kinds of institutions so that they can learn first-hand the challenges, variety, and satisfactions in teaching; PFF illustrates the importance of professional service in a profession that does little to honor or reward service. Moreover, by bringing a diversity of institutions together, PFF provides participants with a comprehensive vision of higher education. And it assists in the development of productive collaborations by involving institutions of all types in the important task of educating the next generation of college professors.

This problem of connecting doctoral study to the realities of jobs is similar for doctoral students planning a career in nonacademic settings, as employers have encouraged internships, research in corporate laboratories, and other ways to let students know what is involved in various kinds of companies. The intensified interest in "nontraditional" positions, e.g., historians to work in museums and local historical organizations and English Ph.D.s to work in publishing houses or journalistic organizations, illustrates a similar need to gain familiarity with a broader array of organizations in which to work. That is why some Preparing Future Faculty programs are also offering Preparing Future Professional programs for students headed for careers outside the academy.

The cultivation of more complete professionals and emphasis on the institutions in which disciplinary expertise is practiced may be the two most important long-term contributions of PFF programs. Regarding calls for change in doctoral education, PFF programs are helping to bring the rhetoric into reality.

Action Recommendations

The overwhelming weight of experience and evidence presented here points to actions that everyone connected with doctoral education can take to improve preparation for an academic career. We know that electronic courses are proliferating, and we know that many businesses and political leaders hope education can be conducted by contracting "professors" who never need to see their students nor interact in a face-to-face setting with them. Nevertheless, colleges and universities should re-commit to full-time faculty. Actions that we recommend to various constituencies involved in graduate education include:

◆ Graduate students interested in exploring a career in the academy should have access to a faculty preparation program. If such a program does not exist at their department or university, students should advocate for it and, if all else fails, design their own individualized experience.

◆ Graduate faculty should take leadership to prepare the doctoral students in their department for the academic—and alternative—careers that are available and seek to understand the real needs and expectations of institutions that are hiring new faculty members.

◆ Leaders of teaching assistant programs should add a faculty preparation component or integrate their work with teaching assistants under the broader rubric of a faculty preparation program.

◆ Doctoral universities and departments should offer a faculty preparation program integrated into the rest of graduate study.

◆ Postdoctoral programs should add teaching and service components and provide experience in diverse institutions for those individuals interested in an academic career.

◆ Colleges and universities that hire new faculty should set comprehensive standards for the faculty they hire, expecting them to present evidence of accomplishment as a teacher and capacity for meaningful professional service as well as the capacity to do research.

◆ Learned societies should make a serious appraisal of post-Ph.D. employment and highlight faculty preparation programs as better ways to prepare for an academic career in their disciplines.

◆ Graduate fellowship providers should require those who receive grant support be involved in a faculty preparation program, rather than simply to complete their studies in a timely manner.

◆ Boards of trustees, state coordinating boards, and accrediting agencies should make a serious appraisal of doctoral programs with an eye toward strengthening the preparation of future faculty.

At a time when teaching, research, and service are in danger of becoming increasingly isolated in faculty life to the detriment of institutional quality, academic leaders must affirm and act upon the conviction that, at their best, faculty perform and integrate these roles. The creation of strong institutions requires that they maintain a commitment to full-time, continuous faculty who can teach effectively, maintain active scholarly minds, and play positive roles in the management of the academic community.

This is an ambitious agenda. But if these recommendations are accepted, we have no doubt that they will help to build the faculty we need for the future. That faculty will be better able to provide a first rate education for future generations of college students and for the benefit of the society.

References

American Association for the Advancement of Science, 1998. Report of new Ph.D.s in fourteen disciplines. Cited in *The Chronicle of Higher Education*, 11 September 1998, A-14 and available on-line at <http://www.nextwave.org/survey/>.

Barr, R. B. and J. Tagg. 1995. From teaching to learning: A new paradigm for undergraduate education. *Change*, November/December, 12–25.

Boyer, E. L. 1990. *Scholarship reconsidered*. Princeton, N.J.: Carnegie Foundation for the Advancement of Teaching.

Boyer Commission on Educating Undergraduates in the Research University. 1998. *Reinventing undergraduate education*. Princeton: Carnegie Foundation for the Improvement of Teaching.

Cerney, J. and M. Nerad. 1997. *Career paths of Ph.D. recipients: First results from the 10 years later study*. Washington, D.C.: Council of Graduate Schools 37th Annual Meeting.

Chickering, A. W. and Z. F. Gamson. 1991. *Applying the seven principles of good practice in undergraduate education*. New directions in teaching and learning, No. 47. San Francisco: Jossey-Bass.

Chism, N. V. and A. S. Pruitt. 1995. Promoting inclusiveness in college teaching. In Wright, W. A. Ed. *Teaching improvement practices: Successful strategies for higher education*. Boston: Anker.

Committee on Graduate Education. 1998. *Report and recommendations*. Washington, D.C.: Association of American Universities.

Committee on Professional Employment. 1997. *Final report*. New York: Modern Language Association.

Committee on Science, Engineering and Public Policy (COSEPUP). 1995. *Reshaping the education of scientists and engineers*. Washington, D.C.: National Academy of Sciences.

DeNeef, L. 1996. *The lessons of PFF concerning the job market*. Preparing Future Faculty Occasional Paper. Washington, D.C.: Association of American Colleges and Universities and Council of Graduate Schools.

Diamond, R. M. and B. E. Adams. 1993. *Recognizing faculty work: Rewards systems for the year 2000*. New Directions in Higher Education, No. 81. San Francisco: Jossey-Bass.

Evans, T. 1997. *Preparing Future Faculty: Lessons learned and next steps.* Association of American Colleges and Universities Annual Meeting, Atlanta.

Finkelstein, M. L., R. K. Seal, and J. H. Schuster. 1998. *The new academic generation.* Baltimore: Johns Hopkins University Press.

Future Professoriate Project. 1993. *Prospectus.* Syracuse, NY: The Graduate School, Syracuse University.

Gaff, J. G. and L. M. Lambert. 1996. Socializing future faculty to the values of undergraduate education. *Change,* July/August, 38–45.

Gaff, J. G. and A. S. Pruitt-Logan. 1998. Preparing college faculty. M.S. Anderson, ed. *The experience of being in graduate school.* New Directions for Higher Education, No. 101. San Francisco: Jossey-Bass.

Gaff, J. G., J. L. Ratcliff, and Associates.1996. *Handbook of the undergraduate curriculum.* San Francisco: Jossey-Bass.

Glassick, C. E., M. T. Huber, and G. I. Maeroff. 1997. *Scholarship assessed.* San Francisco: Jossey-Bass.

Hammonds, J. 1998. Desired characteristics of future community college general education and transfer education faculty: Results of a national delphi study. Unpublished manuscript.

Kennedy, D. 1997. *Academic duty.* Cambridge, MA: Harvard University Press.

Licata, C. M. 1998. Post-Tenure review. *AAHE Bulletin.* Washington, D.C.: American Association for Higher Education, June, 3–6.

McKeachie, W. J. 1998. *Teaching tips.* Boston: Houghton Mifflin.

Marincovich, M., J. Prostko, and F. Stout. 1998. *The professional development of graduate teaching assistants.* Boston: Anker Publishing.

Marsh, H. W. and M. J. Dunkin. 1997. Students' evaluations of university teaching: A multidimensional perspective. In R. P. Perry and J. C. Smart, eds. *Effective teaching in higher education: Research and practice.* New York: Agathon.

Menges, R. J., M. Weimer, and Associates. 1996. *Teaching on solid ground.* San Francisco: Jossey-Bass.

National Research Council. 1998. *Trends in the early careers of life scientists.* Washington, D.C.: National Academy Press.

National Academy of Science. 1996. *The path to the Ph.D.: Measuring graduate attrition in sciences and the humanities.* Washington, D.C.: National Academy Press.

National Science Foundation. 1998. *NSF postdoctoral fellowships in science, mathematics, engineering, and technology education.* Washington, D.C.: National Science Foundation.

National Research Council. 1999. *Survey of earned doctorates.* Washington, D.C.: National Academy Press.

Pascarella, E. T. and P. T. Terenzini. 1991. *How college affects students.* San Francisco: Jossey-Bass.

Presidential Task Force on the Study of Doctoral Education in Chemistry. 1995. *Employment patterns of recent doctorates in chemistry: Institutional perspectives and imperatives for change.* Washington, D.C.: American Chemical Society.

Presidential Young Investigator Colloquium on U.S. Engineering, Mathematics, and Science Education for the Year 2010 and Beyond. 1991. *A vision of the future and recommendations for action for U.S. higher education to assure high quality precollege and undergraduate instruction in engineering, mathematics, and the sciences for everyone.* Washington, D.C.: National Science Foundation.

Pruitt-Logan, A. S., J. G. Gaff, and R. A. Weibl. 1998. *The impact: Assessing the experiences of participants in the preparing future faculty program 1994–1996.* Washington, D.C.: Association of American Colleges and Universities.

Rice, R. E. 1991. The new American scholar: Scholarship and the purposes of the university. *Metropolitan Universities*, 7–18.

Rice, R. E. 1996. *Making a place for the new American scholar.* Washington, D.C.: American Association for Higher Education.

Shine, R. J. 1995. Into the real world: The adventures of a graduate student and PFF. *Liberal Education*, Fall, 36–41.

Shulman, L. S. and P. Hutchings. 1998. *The Carnegie Teaching Academy: The Pew Scholars National Fellowship Program.* Stanford, CA: Carnegie Foundation for the Improvement of Teaching.

Stewart, D. 1994. Graduate education and the preparation of faculty: Path to the future. *CGS Communicator.* Washington, D.C.: Council of Graduate Schools, April.

Tice, S. L., J. G. Gaff, and A. S. Pruitt-Logan. 1998. Preparing Future Faculty Programs: Beyond TA development. In M. Marincovich, J. Prostko, and F. Stout, eds. *The professional development of graduate teaching assistants.* Boston: Anker Publishing.

Appendix

PFF Phase One: Recipients of Major Grants

Arizona State University, with Arizona State University-West, Grand Canyon University, and Maricopa Community College

Howard University, with Bowie State University, the Catholic University of America, Howard Community College, and Marymount University

Northwestern University, with Chicago State University, Lake Forest College, Northeastern Illinois University, and Oakton Community College

University of Minnesota, with the University of Minnesota-Morris, Macalester College, Metropolitan State University, Minneapolis Community College, and Saint Olaf College

University of Washington, with North Seattle Community College, Seattle Central Community College, Seattle Pacific University, Seattle University, the University of Puget Sound, Western Washington University, and the University of Washington-Bothell

PFF Phase One: Recipients of Small Grants

City University of New York Graduate School and University Center, with the Borough of Manhattan Community College, Bronx Community College, Brooklyn College, The City College, Fiorello H. LaGuardia Community College, and Queens College

Cornell University, with Hobart and William Smith Colleges, Ithaca College, and Wells College

Duke University, with Guilford College, Meredith College, and North Carolina Central University

Emory University, with Agnes Scott College, Morehouse College, Oglethorpe University, and Spelman College

Florida State University, with Florida A&M University, Tallahassee Community College, and St. Thomas College

Loyola University of Chicago, with Barat College, College of Lake County, Benedictine University, and Roosevelt University

Marquette University and the *University of Wisconsin-Milwaukee*, with Alverno College, Carthage College, and the University of Wisconsin-Parkside

Northeastern University, with Bunker Hill Community College, Emerson College, Roxbury Community College, and Wentworth Institute of Technology

The Ohio State University, with Capital University, Central State University, Columbus State University, Denison University, and the College of Wooster

University of Cincinnati, with Cincinnati Technical and Community College, College of Mount Saint Joseph, Northern Kentucky University, and Xavier University

University of Kentucky, with Eastern Kentucky University, Kentucky State University, Centre College, and Lexington Community College

University of Texas-Austin, with Austin Community College, Houston-Tillotson College, Saint Edward's University, and Southwest Texas State University

PFF Phase Two

Arizona State University, with Arizona State University-West, Grand Canyon University, and Mesa Community College

Duke University, with Durham Technical Community College, Guilford College, Meredith College, and North Carolina Central University

Florida State University, with Bainbridge College, Florida A&M University, Rollins College, Tallahassee Community College, St. Thomas College, and Valdosta State University

Howard University, with Bowie State University, Howard Community College, Marymount University, The Catholic University of America, and Virginia Tech-Northern Virginia Center

Indiana University-Bloomington, with Anderson College, Butler University, DePauw University, Franklin College, Indiana University-East (Richmond), Indiana University-Indianapolis, Indiana University-Kokomo, Indiana University-Northwest (Gary), Indiana University-Purdue University Fort Wayne, Indiana University-Purdue University at Indianapolis, Indiana University-South Bend, Indiana University-Southeast (Albany), Miami University (OH), Taylor University, the University of Notre Dame, and the University of Kentucky

Marquette University/University of Wisconsin-Milwaukee, with Alverno College, Cardinal Stritch University, Carthage College, Carroll College, Milwaukee Institute of Art and Design, the University of Wisconsin-Green Bay, the University of Wisconsin-Parkside, the University of Wisconsin College at Rock County, the University of Wisconsin College at Washington County, and the University of Wisconsin College at Waukesha County

Northwestern University, with Chicago State University, Lake Forest College, Northeastern Illinois University, and Oakton Community College

Syracuse University, with Colgate University, Hamilton College, LeMoyne College, Onondaga Community College, and the State University of New York-College at Oswego

University of Cincinnati, with the College of Mount Saint Joseph, Northern Kentucky University, the University of Cincinnati-Clermont College, the University of

Cincinnati-College of Applied Sciences, the University of Cincinnati-Raymond Walters College, the University of Cincinnati-University College, and Xavier University

University of Colorado-Boulder, with Colorado School of Mines, Colorado State University, Community College of Denver, Regis University, The Colorado College, the United States Air Force Academy, the University of Colorado-Colorado Springs, and the University of Colorado-Denver

University of Kentucky, with Asbury College, Centre College, Eastern Kentucky University, Kentucky State University, Lexington Community College, and Transylvania University

University of Minnesota, with Augsburg College, Bethel College, College of Saint Catherine, Concordia College, Gustavus Adolphus College, Hamline University, Macalester College, Metropolitan State University, Minneapolis Community and Technical College, St. Olaf College, the University of Minnesota-Duluth, the University of Minnesota-Morris, the University of Saint Thomas, and the University of Wisconsin-River Falls

University of Nebraska-Lincoln, with Chadron State College, Creighton University, Doane College, Grambling State University, Metropolitan Community College, Nebraska Wesleyan University, and the University of Nebraska-Omaha

University of New Hampshire, with Howard University, Keene State University, and Saint Anselm College

University of Washington, with North Seattle Community College, Seattle Central Community College, Seattle Pacific University, Seattle University, the University of Puget Sound, the University of Washington-Bothell, and Western Washington University

PFF Phase Three

American Chemical Society

Duquesne University, with Chatham College, Community College of Allegheny County, La Roche College, Seton Hill College, St. Vincent's College, and Thiel College

CUNY-Queens College, with Queensborough Community College, Baruch College, and Manhattan College

University of California-Los Angeles, with California State University-Fullerton, Mount St. Mary's College, and Mount San Antonio College

University of Massachusetts-Amherst, with Amherst College, Hampshire College, Greenfield Community College, Holyoke Community College, and Smith College

University of Michigan, with Calvin College, Eastern Michigan University, and Grand Valley State University

American Association of Physics Teachers

Howard University, with The Catholic University of America, Bowie State University, Marymount University, Howard Community College, and Virginia Polytechnic Institute and State University/Northern Virginia Campus

University of Arkansas, with the Northwest Arkansas Community College, Crowder College, and the University of Kansas

University of California-San Diego, with San Diego State University, Grossmont Community College, University of San Diego, and San Diego City College.

University of Colorado-Boulder, with University of Northern Colorado, Adams State College, and Laramie County Community College

Special Interest Group on Computer Science Education — Association of Computing Machinery

University of Iowa, with Central College, Grinnell College, Cornell College, and St. Ambrose University

University of Cincinnati, with Xavier University, Northern Kentucky University, and College of Mount Saint Joseph

Mathematical Association of America/American Mathematical Society

Arizona State University, with Arizona State University-West, Grand Canyon University, Northern Arizona University, and Scottsdale Community College

SUNY-Binghamton, with Broome Community College, Ithaca College, King's College, and SUNY- Oneonta

University of Washington, with Seattle University and the Seattle Central Community College

Virginia Polytechnic Institute and State University, with Virginia State University, Washington and Lee University, and Bridgewater College

Biological and Life Science Departments (coordinated by the PFF National Staff)

Duke University, with Durham Technical Community College, Elon College, Guilford College, and Meredith College

University of Cincinnati, with College of Mount Saint Joseph, Northern Kentucky University, Raymond Walter College, and Xavier University

University of South Carolina, with Benedict College, Midlands Technical College, and University of South Carolina at Salkehatchie

University of Nebraska, with Alcorn State University, Creighton University, Dana College, Metropolitan Community College, Grambling State University, University of Nebraska Medical Center, University of Nebraska at Omaha, Nebraska Wesleyan University, and New Mexico Highlands University

PFF Readings and Resources

PFF Occasional Papers

Anderson, H, J. G. Gaff, and A. S. Pruitt-Logan. n.d. *Frequently asked questions about Preparing Future Faculty.* Washington, D.C.: Association of American Colleges and Universities.

Bogle, E., J. A. Blondin, J. L. Miller, and the PFF Staff. November 1997. *Memo to graduate students: Preparing to be the faculty of the future.* Number 5. Washington, D.C.: Association of American Colleges and Universities.

DeNeef, A. L. March 1996. *Lessons of PFF concerning the job market.* Washington, D.C.: Association of American Colleges and Universities.

Gaff, J. G. and A. S. Pruitt. n.d. *Experiences of graduate students, faculty members, and administrators in programs for Preparing Future Faculty: Year one.* Washington, D.C.: Association of American Colleges and Universities.

Pruitt, A. S.. n.d. *The Preparing Future Faculty program and teaching assistant training: Building bridges.* Washington, D.C.: Association of American Colleges and Universities.

Pruitt-Logan, A. S., J. G. Gaff, and R. A. Weibl. May 1998. *The impact: Assessing the experiences of PFF program participants, 1994–1996.* Number 6. Washington, D.C.: Association of American Colleges and Universities.

Tice, S. L. October 1997. *The relationships between faculty preparation programs and teaching assistant development programs.* Number 4. Washington, D.C.: Association of American Colleges and Universities.

PFF Newsletter *In Progress*
  March, 1995, Number 1
  July, 1995, Number 2
  December, 1995, Number 3
  June, 1996, Number 4
  December, 1996, Number 5

Articles, Book Chapters, News Stories

Atwell, R. H. 1996. President's letter. American Council on Education, Washington, D.C., August 30.

Bunce, A. 1996. Small colleges lure profs tired of "publish or perish." *Christian Science Monitor,* February 8.

Cage, M. C. 1996. Learning to teach. *The Chronicle of Higher Education,* February 9, A1, A19–20.

Cody, J. A. and M. E. Hagerman. 1997. Transforming graduate education: A new vision of the professoriate. *Journal of Chemical Education,* 74(5), 525–528.

Gaff, J. G. 1997. The changing roles of faculty and administrators. *Liberal Education,* 83(3), 12–17.

Gaff, J. G. and A. S. Pruitt-Logan. 1998. What happens when we really prepare graduate students to become college professors? In Anderson, M. S. ed. *The experience of being in graduate school: An exploration.* New Directions for Higher Education, Number 101, Spring. San Francisco: Jossey-Bass Publishers.

Gaff, J. G. and L. M. Lambert. 1996. Socializing future faculty to the values of undergraduate education. *Change*, July-August, 38–45.

Gaff, J. G. 1994. Faculty development: The new frontier. *Liberal Education*, 80:4, 16–21.

Hardigg, V. 1995. Back to basics. *U.S. News and World Report: America's Best Graduate Schools*, 70–71.

Herman, R. 1996. A national conversation on doctoral education: An emerging consensus. A Report from the National Convocation on Science and Engineering Doctoral Education. June 15.

Klein, A. 1997. Program gives Ph.Ds a degree of marketability. *The Washington Post*, October 15, B3.

Kreeger, K. 1999. Preparing for changing roles. *The Scientist*, 13:21.

LaPidus, J. B. 1995. Doctoral education and student career needs. In Pruitt, A. S. and P.D. Issac, eds. *Student services for the changing graduate student population*, New Directions for Student Services, Number 72. San Francisco: Jossey-Bass.

Marcus, L. 1996. Learning to teach: Programs prepare graduate students for classrooms. *Chicago Sun Times*, August 6, 1A, 12A–15A.

Mentoring in the scientific community. 1998. *Next Wave: An Electronic Network for the Next Generation of Scientists.* Special Issue, January 9.

Murray, B. 1997. Unique mentor programs bolster students' careers. American Psychological Association *Monitor*, May.

National Research Council. 1999. *Transforming undergraduate education in science, mathematics, engineering, and technology.* Washington, D.C.: National Research Council.

Pruitt, A. S. 1995. Preparing Future Faculty: Frequently asked questions. *CGS Communicator*, April, 10–12.

Pruitt-Logan, A. S. and J. G. Gaff. 1999. Preparing future faculty to focus on diversity. *Diversity Digest.* 4:1, 6–7.

Ransdell, L. B., J. A. Blondin, D. N. Losse and S. Rehling. 1997–98. Preparing doctoral students for faculty roles: The Arizona State University model. *The Journal of Graduate Assistant Development*, 5 (3), 119–124.

Rayson, D., E. L. Farmer and R. Frame. 1999. Preparing Future Faculty: Teaching the academic life. *Perspectives: The American Historical Association Newsletter.* 37(1), 1–13.

Slevin, J. 1992. *The next generation: Preparing graduate students for the professional responsibilities of college teachers.* Washington, D.C.: Association of American Colleges and Universities.

Society for Advancement of Chicanos and Native Americans. 1999. Teaching the teachers: Shaping the preparation of future science and mathematics faculty. *Science (SACNAS) News: A Quarterly Journal*, 3(1), 20.

Stowe, N. J. 1997. Developing a professoriate track for doctoral programs. *Organization of American Historians Newsletter*, 25 (4).

Temple, L. 1998. Colleges learn to ease pressure on grad students. *USA Today*. Wednesday, December 9, 9D.

Temple, L. 1998. Debt, isolation, advisors can break grad students. *USA Today*. Wednesday, December 9, 1D.

Tice, S. L., J. G. Gaff and A. S. Pruitt-Logan. 1998. Preparing Future Faculty programs: Beyond TA development. Marincovich, M., J. Prostco, and F. Stout, eds. *The professional development of graduate teaching assistants: The practitioner's handbook*. Boston: Anker Publishing.

Tillson, L. D. 1998. Developing the professoriate: Today's TAs—tomorrow's tenure track. *The Journal of Graduate Assistant Development*. 5(3), 133–138.

Weisbuch, R. 1999. Six proposals to revive the humanities. *The Chronicle of Higher Education*. 26 March, B4–B5.

Worsfold, V. F. Fall 1997. New priorities for the professoriate: A response to Bruce Busby. *Perspectives: The Journal of the Association for General and Liberal Studies*. 27(2).